IDEAS
General Editor: Jonathan Rée

The Man of Reason

IN THE SAME SERIES

Social Philosophy   *Hans Fink*

Philosophy and the New Physics   *Jonathan Powers*

The Man of Reason

'Male' and 'Female' in
Western Philosophy

GENEVIEVE LLOYD

METHUEN

First published in 1984 by
Methuen & Co. Ltd
11 New Fetter Lane, London EC4P 4EE

© 1984 Genevieve Lloyd

Typeset by Activity Limited, Salisbury, Wilts
Printed in Great Britain by
Richard Clay (The Chaucer Press) Ltd,
Bungay, Suffolk

British Library Cataloguing in Publication Data
Lloyd, Genevieve
    The man of reason.—(Ideas)
    1. Reasoning (Psychology)
    I. Title   II. Series
    128'.3   BF441

    ISBN 0-416-34910-2
    ISBN 0-416-34920-X Pbk

Contents

Acknowledgements		vii
Introduction		viii
1	Reason, science and the domination of matter	1
	Introduction	1
	Femininity and Greek theories of knowledge	2
	Francis Bacon: knowledge as the subjugation of Nature	10
2	The divided soul: manliness and effeminacy	19
	Introduction: Plato on Reason	19
	Philo: 'manly Reason' and the 'entanglements' of sense	22
	Augustine: spiritual equality and natural subordination	28
	Aquinas: 'the principle of the human race' and his 'helpmate'	33
3	Reason as attainment	38
	Introduction	38
	Descartes's method	39
	Hume on Reason and the passions	50

4 Reason and progress 57
   Introduction 57
   Rousseau: the lost youth of the world 58
   Kant: from immaturity to enlightenment 64
   Hegel: Reason as the unfolding of Nature 70
5 The public and the private 74
   Introduction: complementary consciousnesses 74
   Hegel: the feminine nether world 80
6 The struggle for transcendence 86
   Introduction 86
   Hegel: self-consciousness as achievement 88
   Sartre and de Beauvoir: women and transcendence 93
   De Beauvoir on woman as other 96
7 Concluding remarks 103

   Notes 111
   Bibliographical essay 123
   Index 135

Acknowledgements

I wish to thank Kanthi Fernando for typing and word-processing; Catriona Mackenzie for bibliographical assistance; many people for interest and comments on earlier versions, including Rosi Braidotti, John Broomfield, Lorraine Code, Paul Crittenden, Maurita Harney, Brenda Judge, Russell Keat, Evelyn Fox Keller, Kimon Lycos, San MacColl, Carole Pateman, Ross Poole, Amélie Rorty, Tony Skillen, John Small, Michael Stocker. I am especially grateful to Jonathan Rée for inspiration, encouragement and constructive criticism.

Some material from this book has appeared earlier, in similar form, in the following published papers: 'The Man of Reason', *Metaphilosophy*, 10 (1) (1979), 18–37; 'Masters, slaves and others', *Radical Philosophy*, 34 (Summer 1983), 2–8; 'Rousseau on Reason, Nature and Women', *Metaphilosophy*, 14 (3/4) (1983), 308–26; 'Reason, gender and morality in the history of philosophy', *Social Research*, 50 (3) (Autumn 1983), 490–513; 'Public Reason and private passion', *Politics*, 18 (2) (1983), 27–35; 'History of philosophy and the critique of Reason', *Critical Philosophy*, 1 (1) (1984), 5–23.

Introduction

The claim that Reason is 'male', in the context of current philosophical debate, must inevitably conjure up the idea that what is true or reasonable for men might be not at all so for women. Contemporary philosophical concern about our ideals of rationality is, not surprisingly, largely preoccupied with issues of relativism – with the possibility that truth might be relative to particular cultures, or to periods of time. Relativism is a major challenge to Reason's traditional claims to universality – to its capacity to yield ultimately true representations of one real world. In the context of such concern with beliefs and truth, to allege that Reason, despite its pretensions to be gender-free, might after all be thoroughly 'male', may well seem preposterous. To suggest that the celebrated objectivity and universality of our canons of rational belief might not in fact transcend even sexual difference seems to go beyond even the more outrageous versions of cultural relativism. It seems highly implausible to claim that what is true or reasonable varies according to what sex we are. But the implausibility of such 'sexual relativism' can mask other, no less important, respects in which Reason is indeed 'male'.

There is more at stake in assessing our ideals of Reason than questions of the relativity of truth. Reason has figured in western culture not only in the assessment of beliefs, but also in the assessment of character. It is incorporated not just into our criteria of truth, but also into our understanding of what it is to be a person at all, of the requirements that must be met to be a good person, and of the proper relations between our status as knowers and the rest of our lives. Past philosophical reflection on what is distinctive about human life, and on what should be the priorities of a well-lived life, has issued in character ideals centred on the idea of Reason; and the supposed universality and neutrality of these ideals can be seriously questioned. It is with the maleness of these character ideals – the maleness of the Man of Reason – that this book is primarily concerned.

The maleness of the Man of Reason, I will try to show, is no superficial linguistic bias. It lies deep in our philosophical tradition. This is not to say that women have their own truth, or that there are distinctively female criteria for reasonable belief. It is, however, to make a claim which is no less a scandal to the pretensions of Reason. Gender, after all, is one of the things from which truly rational thought is supposed to prescind. Reason is taken to express the real nature of the mind, in which, as Augustine put it, there is no sex. The aspiration to a Reason common to all, transcending the contingent historical circumstances which differentiate minds from one another, lies at the very heart of our philosophical heritage. The conviction that minds, in so far as they are rational, are fundamentally alike underlies many of our moral and political ideals. And the aspiration has inspired, too, our ideals of objective knowledge. The claim, repudiated by relativism, that Reason delivers to us a single objective truth has often been substantiated by appeal to Reason's supposed transcendence of all that differentiates minds from one another.

Our trust in a Reason that knows no sex has, I will argue, been largely self-deceiving. To bring to the surface the implicit maleness of our ideals of Reason is not necessarily to adopt a 'sexual relativism' about rational belief and truth; but it does have important implications for our contemporary understanding of gender difference. It means, for example, that there are not only practical reasons, but also conceptual ones, for the conflicts many women experience between Reason and femininity. The obstacles to female cultivation of Reason spring to a large extent from the fact that our ideals of Reason have historically incorporated an exclusion of the feminine, and that femininity itself has been partly constituted through such processes of exclusion. The historical treatment I will offer of the maleness of Reason bears, too, on the problems of adequately assessing the ideal, current in some contemporary feminist thought, of a distinctively female thought-style. A full treatment of the complexities of these issues lies beyond the scope of this book. What emerges about the historical maleness of Reason, however, does help to illuminate some of the perplexity these questions induce in men and women alike.

1

Reason, science and the domination of matter

Introduction

In a striking passage in *The Second Sex*, Simone de Beauvoir suggested that 'male activity', in prevailing over the 'confused forces of life', has subdued both Nature and woman.[1] The association between Nature and woman to which de Beauvoir here alludes has a long history in the self-definitions of western culture. Nietzsche, with characteristic overstatement, suggested in a fragment on 'The Greek woman' that woman's closeness to Nature makes her play to the State the role that sleep plays for man.

In her nature lies the healing power which replaces that which has been used up, the beneficial rest in which everything immoderate confines itself, the eternal Same, by which the excessive and the surplus regulate themselves. In her the future generation dreams. Woman is more closely related to Nature than man and in all her essentials she remains ever herself. Culture is with her always something external, a something which does not touch the kernel that is eternally faithful to Nature.[2]

But in associating woman with sleep Nietzsche only pushed to its limits a long-standing antipathy between femaleness and active, 'male' Culture. The pursuit of rational knowledge has been a major strand in western culture's definitions of itself as opposed to Nature. It is for us in many ways equatable with Culture's transforming or transcending of Nature. Rational knowledge has been construed as a transcending, transformation or control of natural forces; and the feminine has been associated with what rational knowledge transcends, dominates or simply leaves behind.

Femininity and Greek theories of knowledge

From the beginnings of philosophical thought, femaleness was symbolically associated with what Reason supposedly left behind – the dark powers of the earth goddesses, immersion in unknown forces associated with mysterious female powers. The early Greeks saw women's capacity to conceive as connecting them with the fertility of Nature. As Plato later expressed the thought, women 'imitate the earth'.[3] The transition from the fertility consciousness associated with cults of the earth goddesses to the rites of rational gods and goddesses was legendary in early Greek literature. It was dramatized, for example, in legends of the succession of cults at the site of the oracle at Delphi, incorporated into the prologue of Aeschylus' *Eumenides*, and elaborated as a story of conquest in Euripides' *Iphigenia in Tauris*. Euripides' version presented the transition as a triumph of the forces of Reason over the darkness of the earlier earth mysteries. The infant Apollo slays the Python which guards the old Earth oracle, thereby breaking the power of the

Earth Goddess. She takes revenge by sending up dream oracles to cloud the minds of men with a 'dark dream truth'. But these voices of the night are stilled through the intervention of Zeus, leaving the forces of Reason installed at Delphi. Reason leaves behind the forces associated with female power.[4] What had to be shed in developing culturally prized rationality was, from the start, symbolically associated with femaleness.

These symbolic associations lingered in later refinements of the idea and the ideals of Reason; maleness remained associated with a clear, determinate mode of thought, femaleness with the vague and indeterminate. In the Pythagorean table of opposites, formulated in the sixth century BC, femaleness was explicitly linked with the unbounded – the vague, the indeterminate – as against the bounded – the precise and clearly determined. The Pythagoreans saw the world as a mixture of principles associated with determinate form, seen as good, and others associated with formlessness – the unlimited, irregular or disorderly – which were seen as bad or inferior. There were ten such contrasts in the table: limit/unlimited, odd/even, one/ many, right/left, male/female, rest/motion, straight/curved, light/dark, good/bad, square/oblong. Thus 'male' and 'female', like the other contrasted terms, did not here function as straightforwardly descriptive classifications. 'Male', like the other terms on its side of the table, was construed as superior to its opposite; and the basis for this superiority was its association with the primary Pythagorean contrast between form and formlessness.

Associations between maleness and clear determination or definition persisted in articulations of the form–matter distinction in later Greek philosophical thought. Maleness was aligned with active, determinate form, femaleness with passive, indeterminate matter. The scene for these alignments was set by the traditional Greek understanding of sexual reproduction, which saw the father as providing the formative principle, the real causal force of generation, whilst the mother provided only the matter which received form or determination, and nourished what had been produced by the father. In the

Eumenides, Aeschylus has Apollo exploit this contrast in the affirmation of father-right against mother-right in the moral assessment of Orestes' murder of his mother Clytemnestra, in vengeance of the murder of his father Agamemnon:

> The mother to the child that men call hers
> Is no true life-begetter, but a nurse
> Of live seed. 'Tis the sower of the seed
> Alone begetteth. Woman comes at need,
> A stranger, to hold safe in trust and love
> That bud of her life – save when God above
> Wills that it die.[5]

Plato, in the *Timaeus*,[6] compared the role of limiting form to that of the father, and the role of indefinite matter to the mother; and Aristotle also compared the form–matter relation to that of male and female.[7] This comparison is not of any great significance for either of them in their explicit articulations of the nature of knowledge. But it meant that the very nature of knowledge was implicitly associated with the extrusion of what was symbolically associated with the feminine. To see the implications of this we must look in some detail at the way the form–matter distinction operated in Plato's theory of knowledge.

Knowledge, for Plato, involved a relation within human beings that replicates the relation in the rest of the world between knowable form and unknowable matter. Matching that separation on the side of the knower was a sharp distinction between mind – the principle which understands the rational – and matter, which has no part in knowledge. The knowing mind, like the forms which are its objects, transcends matter. Knowledge involved a correspondence between rational mind and equally rational forms. The idea that the world is itself suffused with Reason was present in much earlier Greek thought, but Plato greatly sophisticated it. In earlier thought, the intelligible object of knowledge was not sharply distinguished from the intelligence which knew it; the notion of *Logos* applied equally to both. Plato recast the idea of the world as mind-imbued in terms of the form–matter distinction; it was only in respect of form that the world was rational. The identification of rational thought and rational universe was not for him an unreflective assumption. It was achieved by deliberately downgrading matter to the realm of the non-rational, fortuitous and disorderly, while preserving for form the correspondence with rational, knowing mind.

In the *Timaeus*, Plato pictured this correspondence as an internalization in human beings of the rational principle in accordance with which the world was fashioned. The relationship of the world-soul to the world is mirrored in that of the rational soul to the body which is subject to it. In the mythology of the *Timaeus*, a cosmic Reason hovers round the sensible world, influencing human minds. Necessity has been subjected to Reason in the creation of the world, and human minds can participate in this Reason. When they do so, they apprehend self-existent ideas, unperceived by sense. Mind, in this special sense, is 'the attribute of the gods and of very few men'.[8]

In the mythology Plato incorporated into the *Timaeus*, there are intimations of a gender differentiation with respect to the exalted conception of cosmic Reason. The reflection of the order and Reason of the universe is supposed to be less clear in the souls of women than in those of men. Their souls originate from the fallen souls of men who were lacking in Reason; hence they are closer to the turbulence of non-rational accretions to the soul. But what is most important for our purposes about Plato's treatment of knowledge is not this, but rather something less explicitly associated with sexual difference. It emerges in his version of mind–matter dualism. Matter, with its overtones of femaleness, is seen as something to be transcended in the search for rational knowledge. It was the relation of master to slave, rather than that of man to woman, that provided the metaphors of dominance in terms of which the Greeks articulated their understanding of knowledge. But this Platonic theme recurs throughout the subsequent history of western thought in ways that both exploit and reinforce the long-standing associations between maleness and form, femaleness and matter.

In his early works, still strongly influenced by Socrates, Plato construed the dualism between intellect and matter as a simple dichotomy between a unitary soul and the body. Here his thought again reflected earlier Greek attitudes to matter. The polarization between body and a supposedly immortal soul figured in the religious rites associated with Orphism and the Pythagorean cults. They conceived the soul as a fallen 'daimon' trapped in a disdained body. This soul was the bearer of humankind's potential divinity. It was reincarnated in a succession of lives until it managed to escape into a god-like immortality; and the process, they thought, could be assisted by the performance of ritual ascetic purifications to purge the soul of gross intrusions of body. Plato transformed these ascetic doctrines, retelling them in terms of the cultivation of Reason; the bearer of immortality became in his version the rational soul, and its freedom from the body was to be gained through the cultivation of rational thought.

In the *Phaedo*, Plato has Socrates, in his speech on his approaching death, present the intellectual life as a purging of the rational soul from the follies of the body.[9] The philosopher's life prepares his soul for release from its prison-house at death. His soul despises the body and flees from it to pursue pure and absolute being with pure intellect alone. Reason enables the soul to go away to the 'pure, and eternal, and immortal, and unchangeable, to which she is akin'. The senses, in contrast, drag the soul back to the realm of the changeable, where she 'wanders about blindly, and becomes confused and dizzy, like a drunken man, from dealing with the things that are ever changing'. The soul which cultivates Reason during life can expect at death to be released from error, folly, fear and fierce passions, living with the 'divine, and the immortal, and the wise'. The soul which does not pursue this 'deliverance and purification' during life is, in contrast, defiled by contact with the body and is at death 'weighed down and dragged back to the visible world', taking root in another body 'like a seed which is sown'. During life, Plato concluded, the god-like rational soul should rule over the slave-like mortal body.

In Plato's later thought, the simplicity of this subjection of body to mind gives way to a more complex location of the non-rational – not outside a soul which is of itself entirely rational, but within the soul as a source of inner conflict. On this later view, the struggle is between a rational part of the soul and other non-rational parts which should be subordinated to it. Later Judaic and Christian thinkers elaborated this Platonic theme in ways that connected it explicitly with the theme of man's rightful domination of woman.

There is another respect in which Plato's use of metaphors of dominance differed from later developments. In his theory, the dominance relation is seen as holding within the knower. The rightful dominance of mind over body, or of superior over inferior aspects of the soul, brings the knower into the required correspondence relations with the forms, which are in turn seen as superior to matter. On this model, knowledge is a contemplation of the eternal forms in abstraction from unknowable, non-rational matter. The symbolism of dominance and subordination occurs in the articulation of the process by which knowledge is gained. Knowledge itself is not seen as a domination of its objects, but as an enraptured contemplation of them.

Plato's picture has been highly influential in the formation of our contemporary ways of thinking about knowledge. But overlaid on it is a very different way of construing knowledge in terms of dominance – the model which receives its most explicit formulation, and has its most explicit associations with the male–female distinction, in the seventeenth century in the thought of Francis Bacon. On this model, knowledge itself is construed as a domination of Nature. This brings with it a different understanding of knowledge and its objects. To see the significance of the change it will be helpful first to look briefly at the transformation of Plato's version of the form–matter distinction in the thought of Aristotle.

Aristotle transformed Plato's form–matter distinction and its role in theory of knowledge; and with this transformation, the mind–body relationship also underwent a crucial change. In the *Metaphysics*, Aristotle hailed Plato's sophistication of the notion of form as a great advance over the primitive pre-Socratic cosmologies, which equated the basic principles of things with a single material element.[10] Plato's formal principles, Aristotle commented, were rightly set apart from the sensible. But he repudiated Plato's development of this insight into a dualism between a realm of change, apprehended through the senses, and a different realm of eternal forms. Aristotle brought the forms down from their transcendent realm to become the intelligible principles of changing, sensible things. The formal remains, for him, the proper object of necessary knowledge, and it is attained by the exercise of a purely intellectual faculty. But it is now grasped in the particular and sensible; it does not – as it did for Plato – escape into a distinct, supersensible realm. In Aristotle's own system, a dualism remained between what is sensed and what is grasped by Reason. But it no longer coincided with a distinction between changeable, created material things and uncreated, timeless, non-material forms. Aristotelian forms can function as intelligible principles of material things; and where they do, it is only in conjunction with matter that they can be regarded as existing at all. The mind–body relationship was accordingly transformed in the Aristotelian philosophy. The rational soul became the form of the body, and hence was no longer construed as the presence in human beings of a divine stuff which really belongs elsewhere. It was the intelligible principle of the body, not its prisoner; and rational knowledge was no longer construed as the soul's escape from the body.

What is for our purposes significant in Aristotle's transformation of Plato's notion of form is highlighted in Aquinas's treatment, in the *Summa Theologica*, of the Platonic version of scientific knowledge.[11] On his diagnosis, Plato overreached himself in his desire to save the certitude of intellect from the encroachment of the uncertainty of the senses. By introducing a special sphere of changeless forms as the proper object of scientific knowledge, he removed 'whatever appertains to the act of intellect' from the material world altogether – a self-defeating move, since it excludes knowledge of matter and movement from science. Moreover, Aquinas suggests, it seems ridiculous to explain knowledge of sensible substances by knowledge of things altogether different. Plato's mistake, he thinks, was to take too far his idea of knowledge as a kind of similitude. It is not necessary that the form of the thing known be in the knower in the same manner as in the object. It occurs in the intellect under conditions of universality, immateriality and immobility. But from this it does not, as Plato thought, follow that the things we understand must have in themselves an existence under the same conditions of immateriality and immobility. Changing material things are themselves genuinely known. Although the soul, through intellect, knows bodies by a knowledge which is immaterial, universal and necessary, 'there is nothing to hinder our having an immovable science of movable things'.

The Aristotelian *rapprochement* of form and matter thus makes it possible for changeable material things to be proper objects of genuine knowledge. But within the Aristotelian framework this does not change the basic model of knowledge as a contemplation of forms. The form–matter distinction continues to operate, although it now holds within each object. Knowledge still involves the abstraction from matter of formal, intelligible principles, although these are no longer seen as located in a different realm from the sensible. The paradigm of knowledge is still the contemplation by a rational mind of something inherently mind-like, freed of matter.

Against the background of these contrasts, within a broader similarity, between the Platonic and Aristotelian views of knowledge, we can now see the significance of Bacon. In his thought, the gap between form and matter is completely closed. The split between knowable forms and unknowable matter is repudiated; and with it the model of knowledge as contemplation of forms. With this change, both the theme of dominance and the male–female distinction enter quite different relations with knowledge.

Francis Bacon: knowledge as the subjugation of Nature

Bacon construed the mind's task in knowledge not as mere contemplation, but as control of Nature. This demanded a reconstruction of the proper objects of knowledge, bypassing the distinction between forms and matter. Forms – whether they be transcendent Platonic entities or Aristotelian abstract intelligible principles of material things – are appropriate objects of knowledge construed on a contemplative model. But if knowledge is construed as an instrument of control of Nature, its proper objects must be something more readily conceived as manipulable. Bacon's repudiation of the notion of form is thus closely connected with his conception of knowledge as power.

The only 'forms' Bacon was prepared to countenance as objects of scientific knowledge had very different relations to matter from those envisaged by either Plato or Aristotle. 'It is manifest,' he wrote in *The Advancement of Learning*, that Plato, 'a man of a sublime genius, who took a view of everything as from a high rock, saw in his doctrine of ideas that "forms were the true object of knowledge".' But he 'lost the advantage of this just opinion by contemplating and grasping at forms totally abstracted from matter, and not as determined in it.'[12] Bacon's closing of the gap between forms and matter went much further than that of Aristotle, amounting in effect to a total obliteration of the distinction. To understand physical nature, we must rather consider 'matter, its conformation, and the changes of that conformation, its own action, and the law of this action or motion; for forms are a mere fiction of the human mind, unless you will call the laws of action by that name'.[13] The understanding of physical Nature became for Bacon an understanding of the patterns in which matter is organized in accordance with mechanical laws. The importance of this change goes beyond the progress of scientific knowledge.

In this new picture, the material world is seen as devoid of mind, although, as a product of a rational creator, it is orderly and intelligible. It conforms to laws that can be understood; but it does not, as the Greeks thought, contain mind within it. Nature is construed not by analogy with an organism, containing its intelligible principles of motion within it, but rather by analogy with a machine: as object of scientific knowledge, it is understood not in terms of intelligible principles enforming matter, but as mechanism. Bacon thus repudiated the model of knowledge as a correspondence between rational mind and intelligible forms, with its assumption that pure intellect could not distort reality. There are, he thinks, errors which 'cleave to the nature of the understanding'. 'For however men may amuse themselves, and admire, or almost adore the mind, it is certain, that like an irregular glass, it alters the rays of things, by its figure, and different intersections.'[14] The sceptics, rather than mistrusting the senses, should have mistrusted the 'errors and obstinacy of the mind', which refuses to obey the nature of things.[15] The mind itself should be seen as 'a magical glass, full of superstitions and apparitions'. The perceptions of the mind, no less than those of the senses, 'bear reference to man and not to the universe'.[16] Nature cannot be expected to conform to the ideas the mind finds within itself when it engages in pure intellectual contemplation. Knowledge must be painstakingly pursued by attending to Nature; and this attending cannot be construed in terms of contemplation.

Bacon, notoriously, used sexual metaphors to express his idea of scientific knowledge as control of a Nature in which form and matter are no longer separated. In Greek thought, femaleness was symbolically associated with the non-rational, the disorderly, the unknowable – with what must be set aside in the cultivation of knowledge. Bacon united matter and form – Nature as female and Nature as knowable. Knowable Nature is presented as female, and the task of science is the exercise of the right kind of male domination over her. 'Let us establish a chaste and lawful marriage between Mind and Nature,' he writes.[17] The right kind of nuptual dominance, he insists, is not a tyranny. Nature is 'only to be commanded by obeying her'.[18] But it does demand a degree of force: 'nature betrays her secrets more fully when in the grip and under the pressure of art than when in enjoyment of her natural liberty.'[19] The expected outcome of the new science is also expressed in sexual metaphors. Having established the right nuptual relationship, properly expressed in a 'just and legitimate familiarity betwixt the mind and things',[20] the new science can expect a fruitful issue from this furnishing of a 'nuptual couch for the mind and the universe'. From the union can be expected to spring 'assistance to man' and a 'race of discoveries, which will contribute to his wants and vanquish his miseries'.[21] The most striking of these sexual metaphors are in an early, strangely strident work entitled *The Masculine Birth of Time*. 'I am come in very truth', says the narrator in that work, 'leading to you Nature with all her children to bind her to your service and make her your slave.'[22]

> My dear, dear boy, what I purpose is to unite you with *things themselves* in a chaste, holy and legal wedlock; and from this association you will secure an increase beyond all the hopes and prayers of ordinary marriages, to wit, a blessed race of Heroes or Supermen who will overcome the immeasurable helplessness and poverty of the human race, which cause it more destruction than all giants, monsters or tyrants, and will make you peaceful, happy, prosperous and secure.[23]

None of the elements of Bacon's account of knowledge is new. The idea that man has a rightful dominion – linked with his capacity for knowledge – over the rest of Nature goes back to the Genesis story, with reference to which Bacon named his *Great Instauration*. The proper direction of the arts and sciences, once the distortions of earlier false philosophies have been shed, is supposed to restore to man this rightful dominion lost through his original sin of pride. We have already seen the theme of mind's domination of matter in Plato's picture of knowledge as involving the subjection of the slave-like body to the soul. And the personification of Nature as female is no innovation. But Bacon brings all this together in a powerful new model of knowledge. The dominance relation – rather than holding between mind and body, or within the mind between different aspects of mental functioning – now holds between mind and Nature as the object of knowledge. Knowledge is itself the domination of Nature.

Today, Bacon's metaphors for the new science are inevitably seen in the light of contemporary preoccupations with the more negative aspects of science construed as human domination of Nature. But from his own perspective what is salient about the metaphors is quite different. They spring from a vision of the positive virtues of the new approach to science: the emphasis on sensory observation and experiment, the conviction that only an attentive observation of Nature, in conjunction with testing through experiments, will yield genuine knowledge. And they express the intellectual ideals which Bacon saw as implicit in this new science. These frequently disconcerting metaphors express two main points: first, that he who would know Nature must turn away from mere ideas and abstractions and painstakingly attend to natural phenomena; and, second, that this painstaking attention cannot be regarded as mere contemplation. Earlier philosophies, Bacon complains, being concerned with 'mere abstractions', only 'catch and grasp' at Nature, never 'seize or detain her'.[24] The Aristotelian philosophy has 'left Nature herself untouched and inviolate'; Aristotle 'dissipated his energies in comparing, contrasting and analysing popular notions about her'.[25] Bacon's demystified forms are always determined in matter, and understanding them is inseparable from the control and manipulation of Nature, although the practical and the speculative can, for convenience, be considered apart. This theme of the interconnections between knowledge and power is Bacon's main contribution to our ways of thinking about mind's relation to the rest of Nature. It is worth looking at it in more detail.

Philosophy, Bacon complains in the opening pages of *The Great Instauration*, has 'come down to us in the person of master and scholar, instead of inventor and improver'.[26] His own aim is not only the 'contemplative happiness', but the 'whole fortunes, and affairs, and powers, and works of men'. Man is both 'minister' and 'interpreter' of Nature; whence 'those twin intentions, human knowledge and human power, are really coincident'.[27] The speculative and the practical are distinguished from one another only as 'the search after causes' and 'the production of effects'; and these are in fact inseparable. The natural philosopher, as well as being a 'miner', digging out what lies concealed, also has the office of 'smelter'.[28] To understand forms is to be able to superinduce new natures on matter, which is the labour and aim of human power. Even that part of knowledge which may seem most remote from action – the understanding of forms – is ennobled by its role in releasing human power and leading it into an 'immense and open field of work'.[29]

The more we understand, the better our prospects of changing things; and these interconnections between knowledge and power are for Bacon so close as to amount to an identity. Truth and utility are equated, though not in a narrowly short-term utilitarian spirit. We should, Bacon urges, look for experiments that will 'afford light rather than profit',[30] confident in the expectation of long-term results from the better understanding of Nature. With that proviso understood, the 'practical' and the 'theoretical' are in fact the same: 'that which is most useful in practice is most correct in theory.'[31] The right analogy for the ideal science, then, is neither the activity of the ants, who merely heap up and use their store, nor that of the spiders, spinning out their webs; but rather that of the bee, who 'extracts matter from the flowers of the garden and the field, but works and fashions it by its own efforts'.[32] Practical results are not only the means to improve human well-being; they are the guarantee of truth.

> The rule of religion, that a man should show his faith by his works, holds good in natural philosophy too. Science also must be known by works. It is by the witness of works, rather than by logic or even observation, that truth is revealed and established. Whence it follows that the improvement of man's mind and the improvement of his lot are one and the same thing.[33]

Seeing Bacon's equation of knowledge and power in this wider context highlights something which from our own historical perspective seems strange – that for Bacon the linking of knowledge with power was a return from the arrogance of earlier philosophies to intellectual humility. This is what his sexual metaphors are meant to convey. The control of Nature through science returns to man the rightful dominion which he lost through the sin of pride; and this dominion is regained precisely through the intellectual humility encapsulated in the new science. For Bacon, the endeavour to 'renew and enlarge the power and empire of mankind in general over the universe'[34] is a sound and noble ambition, involving chastity, restraint and respect, not only on the part of Nature as chaste wife, but also on the part of her suitors. We have no right to expect Nature to come to us: 'Enough if, on our approaching her with due respect, she condescends to show herself.'[35] It is pride that has 'brought men to such a pitch of madness that they prefer to commune with their own spirits rather than with the spirit of nature'.[36] It is through pride, through wanting to be like gods, following the dictates of our own reason, that humanity has forfeited its rightful dominion over nature through true and solid arts.

> Wherefore, if there be any humility towards the Creator, if there be any praise and reverence towards his works: if there be any charity towards men, and zeal to lessen human wants and sufferings; if there be any love of truth in natural things, any hatred of darkness, any desire to purify the understanding; men are to be entreated again and again that they should dismiss for a while, or at least put aside, those inconstant and preposterous philosophies which prefer theses to hypotheses, have led experience captive, and triumphed over the works of God; that they should humbly and with a certain reverence draw near to the book of Creation; that they should there make a stay, that on it they should meditate, and that then washed and clean they should in chastity and integrity turn them from opinion. This is that speech and language which has gone out to all the ends of the earth, and has not suffered the confusion of Babel; this men must learn again, and,

resuming their youth, they must become again as little children and deign to take its alphabet into their hands.[37]

But whatever may have been Bacon's conscious intent in describing scientific knowledge in terms of the male–female distinction, its upshot was to build a new version of the transcending of the feminine into the very articulation of the nature of science – this time with the emphasis on the malleability and tractability of matter. Matter is no longer seen as what has to be dominated in order to *attain* knowledge, but as the proper object of knowledge – now construed as the power to manipulate and transform. Malleability, rather than the eternal unchangeability of the forms, is the crucial feature of the objects of Baconian science. But this repudiation of the unknowability of matter did not shake the grip of earlier symbolic antitheses between femaleness and the activity of knowledge. On the contrary, it gave them a new and more powerful expression.

The transcending of the feminine was not an explicit feature of Greek theories of knowledge in their original form. But it was associated with knowledge through implicit associations of femaleness with matter, which pure intellect was supposed to transcend. Mind's domination of matter, as we have seen, was not explicitly associated with the male–female distinction, but rather with the master–slave relation. Early Greek associations of femaleness with matter did, none the less, influence the ways in which these theories of knowledge affected the philosophical imagination in later developments of the tradition. And in Bacon's metaphors the control of the feminine became explicitly associated with the very nature of knowledge.

How deep is the maleness of Bacon's expression of the nature of the new science? It may seem that it operates at a relatively superficial level. It is true that he unreflectively utilized associations between Nature and femaleness which abounded in his cultural tradition; and much of the content of his thought, as we have seen, can be explicated without the sexual metaphors. But the problem cannot be remedied by simply shedding superficial literary embellishments. The intellectual virtues involved in being a good Baconian scientist are articulated in terms of the right male attitude to the feminine: chastity, respect and restraint. The good scientist is a gallant suitor. Nature is supposed to be treated with the respect appropriate to a femininity overlaid with long-standing associations with mystery – an awe, however, which is strictly contained. Nature is mysterious, aloof – but, for all that, eminently knowable and controllable. The metaphors do not merely express conceptual points about the relations between knowledge and its objects. They give a male content to what it is to be a good knower.

Both kinds of symbolism – the Greeks' unknowable matter, to be transcended in knowledge, and Bacon's mysterious, but controllable Nature – have played crucial roles in the constitution of the feminine in relation to our ideals of knowledge. The theme of the dominance of mind over body, or of intellect over inferior parts of the soul, was developed, as we will see in the next chapter, in medieval versions of character ideals associated with maleness. And Bacon's connection of knowledge with power was developed in later ideas of Reason and progress.

2

The divided soul: manliness and effeminacy

Introduction: Plato on Reason

In Book IV of the *Republic*, Plato tells an illustrative tale of conflict within the human soul.[1] Leontius, when he comes across some dead bodies lying near an executioner, feels a desire to look at them, but also disgust, which makes him turn aside. For some time he fights with himself, covering his eyes with his hand. But in the end his desire gets the better of him; opening his eyes wide with his fingers, he runs to the bodies, saying, 'There you are, curse you, have your fill of the lovely spectacle.' Reason here struggles to control the desire to look, and loses the struggle. But there is no doubt where the rights of victory lie; and the 'spiritedness' of anger sides with Reason, deploring the outcome.

Imagery of power struggles, dominance and subjection abounds in philosophical accounts of the conflicts within human nature. We saw it in a simple form in Plato's treatment of knowledge in the *Phaedo*. Intellect, the superior god-like aspect of human beings, ought to dominate the slave-like body; and knowledge achieves this matching between the subjection of the body and the wider subjection of matter to the eternal forms. But this early Platonic model of the place of intellect in the well-lived life was a simplistic one in comparison with the more subtle model of a divided soul which replaced it in his later thought. In the early model, Plato described the whole soul as the domain of Reason, and presented the non-rational as an alien intrusion from body. The life of Reason was a spurning of the gross intrusions of bodily perturbation. In Plato's later thought, the soul ceased to be a sovereign territory from whose borders non-rational forces were to be expelled. It became a divided soul, within which Reason must contend with non-rational human qualities which are no less properly parts of the soul. The change allowed a richer and subtler presentation of Reason's relations with the non-rational – and of the role of intellect in the well-lived life – than the earlier simple dualism between intellect and body. In the story of Leontius, spirited anger is no alien perturbation from body, but an ally of Reason.

   The role of such passions in the good life is elaborated in other Platonic dialogues. In the *Philebus*, Plato has Socrates ask whether anyone of us would consent to live 'having wisdom and mind and knowledge and memory of all things, but having no sense of pleasure or pain, and wholly unaffected by these and the like feelings'.[2] The approved reply is that the life which combines pleasure with mind and wisdom is the better life. In the *Phaedrus*, Plato offered an even more positive account of the role of desire and passion in the good life.[3] The theme is introduced in the context of an argument about whether a young man is better advised to accept a suitor not frenzied by the emotional turmoil and jealous torments of sexual attraction – a lover who can offer, rather, a calm rational attention to the youth's own interests. Preference for such a non-passionate love, Socrates argues, rests on a false division. It fails to carve the beast of reality according to the natural formation, where the joint is; it hacks it, breaking its natural parts as a bad carver might. His opponent has recognized only a single form of unreason – the kind that is an infirmity – and has located love as a species within it. The right division recognizes not only this destructive form of love, but another kind – a divine frenzy which impels the soul through the pursuit of knowledge to an immortal joy. This love is a form of madness, but also a divine gift – a release of the soul from the yoke of custom and convention. The beauty which inspires it reminds the soul of its previous non-bodily contemplation of changeless forms. Such love is an agitation of the soul – a 'growing of wings' in eager anticipation of its flight to the realm of the gods. If properly used, it will bring the soul to a state greatly superior to anything it can have from the calm non-passionate pursuit of rational prudence alone. The attraction to fleshly beauty thus has two forms – one gross and vicious, the other noble, but no less frenzied – and the two are in conflict in the lover's soul.

All this made possible an enrichment of Plato's conception of Reason. The cultivation of Reason remained at the centre of the Platonic life-style, but non-intellectual elements were now incorporated into the life of the soul, as energizing psychic forces on which Reason draws. On the other hand, it also complicated Reason's struggle for purity. Both aspects of the divided-soul model emerge in the *Phaedrus* metaphor of the soul as a pair of winged horses, joined together in natural union with their charioteer.[4] One horse is white, noble and easily guided; the other is a dark, crooked, lumbering animal, shag-eared and deaf, hardly yielding to whip and spur. The contrasted behaviour of the two horses makes the management of the human chariot a difficult and anxious task. Within this unified complex the noble horse, like 'spiritedness' in the Leontius story, is an ally of the rational guiding principle – represented by the charioteer – answering readily to its checks and admonitions. The ignoble horse, in contrast, fights back against the restraining force of the charioteer and can be controlled only with extreme difficulty. The chariot is put into violent perturbation by the conflict between the brutish beast's desire to rush on to enjoy and beget in response to the sight of beauty, and the amazed rapture of the noble horse – in alliance with the charioteer – at the same sight. This conflict of desires is intrinsic to passionate love. But its favourable resolution, Socrates argues, is of much more benefit to the beloved than anything he can hope to gain from the attentions of a disinterested, passionless suitor. The beloved catches the divine frenzy from his lover and the experience of being the object of this passionate love is itself a point of entry to the intellectual life – the love of wisdom.

The later Plato thus saw passionate love and desire as the beginning of the soul's process of liberation through knowledge; although it must first transcend its preoccupation with mere bodily beauty, moving through a succession of stages to love of the eternal forms. In the *Symposium*, Plato elaborates the interconnections between love, in its various forms, and knowledge. The wise woman Diotima, Socrates' instructor in the art of love, tells him that although the name 'love' has been appropriated to one particular form of desire, its great and subtle power really encompasses all desire of good and happiness.[5] Love's aim is birth in beauty, whether of body or soul. This aim in all its forms expresses mortal nature's longing for immortality; and knowledge is one of these forms. It is through being a form of love that knowledge is connected with immortality. The pursuit of wisdom is a spiritual procreation, which shares with physical procreation the desire for immortality through generation – the desire to leave behind a new and different existence in place of the 'old worn-out mortality'. The pursuit of wisdom thus shares a common structure with physical procreation; but its aim is a superior form of immortality. Men who are 'pregnant in the body only' betake themselves to women and beget children. But there are men who are 'more creative in their soul than in their bodies, creative of that which it is proper for the soul to conceive and bring forth – wisdom and virtue'.

Diotima presents the art of love as a progression, moving from love of the particular to love of the general, and ascending from earthly beauty to the 'life which above all others a man should love, in the contemplation of beauty absolute'. The end result is similar to the culmination of moral progress in the *Phaedo*. The lover progresses to the contemplation of a divine beauty, 'not infected by the pollutions of the flesh and all the colours and vanities of mortal life'. But in Diotima's version of the lover's progress Reason does not simply shed the perturbations of passion, but assimilates their energizing force. Reason itself becomes a passionate faculty and a creative, productive one. The lover of wisdom brings forth 'not images of beauty, but realities'; he produces and nourishes true virtue. The Platonic lover – the philosopher – 'gives birth in beauty'. Love is generative, and Platonic wisdom is its highest form. The old conflicts between Reason and the transcended fertility mysteries are here subsumed in a treatment of Reason as itself generative.

The divided-soul model, when it is later brought into conjunction with male–female symbolism, produces much more complex relationships between femininity and Reason than the alignments of femaleness and matter, maleness and Reason, discussed in Chapter 1. I will now look at three versions of this, presented by Philo, Augustine and Aquinas. All three attempted to harmonize Judaeo-Christian theology with Greek philosophy. Their use of male–female symbolism to describe Reason occurs in a context of interpretation of the Genesis stories of Eve's subsidiary creation out of Adam's side, her subordination to Adam, and her role as temptress in his fall.

Philo: 'manly Reason' and the 'entanglements' of sense

Philo, an Alexandrian Jew, writing in the first century AD, used Greek philosophical models in interpreting Jewish scriptures. Echoing Plato, he described sense-perception as the source of the disorders of the soul, giving rise to a tide of passions which threatens to engulf sovereign Reason. And he allegorized the destructive effects of sense-perception in a remarkable synthesis of the Genesis account of relations between the sexes with a Platonic treatment of Reason's corruption through the senses.[6] Reason rules in a divided soul over inferior sense-perception and the desire and passions it breeds for sensory objects. Philo presents the dire consequences of the reversal of this proper relation in a passage that is packed with images of dominance and subjection in his work *On the Virtues*.

Most profitless is it that Mind should listen to Sense-perception, and not Sense-perception to Mind: for it is always right that the superior should rule and the inferior be ruled; and Mind is superior to Sense-perception. When the chariot-eer is in command and guides the horses with the reins, the chariot goes the way he wishes, but if the horses have become unruly and got the upper hand, it has often happened that the charioteer has been dragged down and that the horses have been precipitated into a ditch by the violence of their motion, and that there is a general disaster. A ship, again, keeps to her straight course, when the helmsman grasping the tiller steers accordingly, but capsizes when a contrary wind has sprung up over the sea, and the surge has settled in it. Just so, when Mind, the charioteer or helmsman of the soul, rules the whole living being as a governor does a city, the life holds a straight course, but when the irrational sense gains the chief place, a terrible confusion overtakes it, just as when slaves have risen against their masters: for then, in very deed, the mind is set on fire and is all ablaze, and that fire is kindled by the objects of sense which Sense-perception supplies.[7]

In Philo's retelling of the Genesis story, woman, symbolizing sense-perception, is the source of the Fall for man, symbolizing Mind. Sense-perception, like woman, was created to be a 'helper and ally' of Mind. The order of God's creation in the Genesis story reflects the rightful priorities among the human faculties: 'first He made mind, the man, for mind is most venerable in a human being; then bodily sense, the woman, then after them in the third place pleasure.'[8] Like woman too, however, sense-perception turns out to be the source of man's wretchedness – of the fall into 'that fleeting and mortal existence which is not an existence but a period of time full of misery'. Prompted by a 'mind devoid of steadfastness and firm foundation', woman, as sense-perception, falls prey to the wiles of the serpent, symbolizing pleasure.[9] That the Genesis story has pleasure tempt man through woman is, Philo says, a 'telling and well-made point'. For in us 'mind corresponds to man, the senses to woman; and pleasure encounters and holds parley with the senses first, and through them cheats with her quackeries, the sovereign mind itself.'[10]

Mind and sense-perception come together for the apprehension of physical objects. But the perturbations of bodily pleasures ensue, and with them the 'life of mortality and wretchedness in lieu of that of immortality and bliss'.[11] Philo's uses of allegory are often illuminating about the conceptual relations between mind and sense-perception. But they also forge powerful symbolic connections between male–female relations and ideas of the rightful ordering of different aspects of human nature; and powerful symbolic connections, too, between gender and the priorities of a well-lived life. When Mind becomes the slave, warns Philo, it abandons God and becomes one with sense-perception.

> Observe that it is not the woman that cleaves to the man, but conversely the man to the woman. Mind to Sense-perception. For when that which is superior, namely Mind, becomes one with that which is inferior, namely Sense-perception, it resolves itself into the order of the flesh which is inferior, into Sense-perception, the moving cause of the passions. But if Sense the inferior follow Mind the superior, there will be flesh no more, but both of them will be Mind.[12]

The old Greek theme of female passivity is also incorporated into Philo's allegorization: 'just as the man shows himself in activity and the woman in passivity, so the province of the mind is activity, and that of the perceptive sense passivity, as in woman.'[13]

That woman symbolically represents the non-rational aspects of human nature does not of itself carry the implication that women are irrational, but it is precisely his pejorative attitude to women that enables Philo's allegories to function as they do. Philo's use of male–female symbolism and his depreciation both of actual women and of sense-perception are so closely intertwined that often no clear separation can be made between them. His rather chaotic list of 'distinctions of existence' in the *Allegorical Interpretation* partly echoes the Pythagorean table of opposites:

> lifeless, living; irrational, rational; good, bad; slave, free; young, or older; male, female; foreign, or native; sickly, healthy; maimed, entire; so in the soul too there are lifeless, incomplete, diseased, enslaved, female, and countless other movements full of disabilities; and on the other hand movements living, entire, male, free, sound, elder, good, genuine, and, in a real sense, of the fatherland.[14]

And these pejorative associations of femaleness are both exploited and reinforced by Philo's allegories. The interplay between the literal and the allegorical can be seen in a passage in the *Special Laws*, where Philo cites with approval an allegorical interpretation of the Judaic penalty of cutting off a woman's hand for such curious offences as 'clutching opponents' genitals in the market place':

> There is in the soul a male and female element just as there is in families, the male corresponding to the men, the female to the women. The male soul assigns itself to God alone as the Father and Maker of the Universe and the Cause of all things. The female clings to all that is born and perishes; it stretches out its faculties like a hand to catch blindly at what comes in its way, and gives the clasp of friendship to the world of created things with all its numberless changes and transmutations, instead of to the divine order, the immutable, the blessed, the thrice happy.[15]

Philo's slides between literal and symbolic versions of the theme of female irrationality are compounded by the fact that, as well as associating femaleness with the non-rational aspects of human nature, he also uses woman as a symbol of the material world, which 'drags down' the human soul. Mind, strictly, is supposed to transcend the sexual division. It belongs to the incorporeal realm which is neither male nor female. But it is sense-perception that drags down this supposedly asexual mind, made in God's image; and the appearance in the soul of the sense-perceptible material world is symbolized as female, while maleness, in contrast, symbolically represents the sphere of Mind and God himself. Thus maleness occurs symbolically in the system in two ways: once within the material world, as human mind in contrast to sense-perception; but also as identified with the transcendent asexual realm. And femaleness likewise occurs twice: once within the material world as sense-perception in contrast to male mind; but also as equated with the material world itself, as against the transcendent realm of Mind.[16]

This kind of symbolic fluctuation is only to be expected in such an allegorical exercise. The male–female symbolism can be used to convey more than one contrast between superiors and inferiors; and Philo exploits its potential to the full. But these uses of the male–female symbolism come together to make the path of spiritual progress through the cultivation of mind only ambivalently available to women. Moral progress, for Philo as for Plato, involves mind's transcending the corrupting influences of sense-perception and bodily passion. Against the background of his allegorizations, this becomes a struggle to transcend the feminine. The virtuous life, in which Reason gains its rightful supremacy over the lower aspects of human nature, comes through as a process of, as it were, becoming male – shedding the influence and intrusion of femaleness. Human beings are urged to leave behind the 'weak feminine passion of sense-perception' and to give forth 'as incense' the 'manly reasoning schooled in fortitude'.[17] Progress, says Philo, 'is indeed nothing else than the giving up of the female gender by changing into the male, since the female gender is material, passive, corporeal and sense-perceptible, while the male is active, rational, incorporeal and more akin to mind and thought.'[18] The passions themselves are 'by nature feminine', and we must practise the quitting of these for the masculine traits that mark the 'noble affections'.[19]

This version of moral progress is not meant to exclude actual women, but it calls on them to set aside those character traits which are supposed to characterize them as female. For a male, in contrast, progress is a matter of strengthening traits which are already symbolically associated with maleness: 'when God begins to consort with the soul, He makes what before was a woman into a virgin again, for He takes away the degenerate and emasculate passions which unmanned it and plants instead the native growth of unpolluted virtues.'[20] For either sex, spiritual progress involves shedding the passivity associated with femaleness to emphasize the active strengths associated with maleness.

> The male is more complete, more dominant than the female, closer akin to causal activity, for the female is incomplete and in subjection and belongs to the category of the passive rather than the active. So too with the two ingredients which constitute our life-principle, the rational and the irrational; the rational which belongs to mind and reason is of the masculine gender, the irrational, the province of sense, is of the feminine. Mind belongs to a genus wholly superior to sense as man is to woman.[21]

The 'man of knowledge' actively engages with his sorrows, 'stepping out like an athlete to meet all grievous things with strength and robust vigour'.[22] Women are not actually excluded from the moral athleticism of men of knowledge, but they can achieve it only at the cost of what specifically defines their femininity.

The obstacles Philo's women face in being virtuous spring from the male–female symbolism. But they are not merely symbolic obstacles. The symbols have real effects on the way women are understood with respect to Reason. Philo's allegorical linkings of gender and the elements of a divided human nature cannot be dismissed as inconsequential, fantastic plays on associated ideas. He himself took them seriously; allegories for him – and for many later thinkers influenced by him – were no mere stylistic embellishments, but serious vehicles of textual interpretation. Philo warned against treating the Genesis stories themselves as mere 'mythical fictions' such as 'poets and sophists' delight in. They are, he insists, 'modes of making ideas visible, bidding us resort to allegorical interpretations guided in our rendering by what lies beneath the surface'.[23] His own 'allegorical interpretations' are no less serious in intent, and no less significant in their influence. Arbitrary and fanciful as his allegories may now appear, the ideas and ideals articulated through them became deeply engrained in the developing structures of thought about Reason and gender.

Augustine: spiritual equality and natural subordination

The use of male–female symbolism to express subordination relations between elements of a divided human nature continued in the Christian tradition of biblical exegesis. By the fourth century, Augustine was able to locate his own explication of the Genesis story against the background of a prolific tradition of allegorical interpretations relating to gender difference; his version of the exercise is important and interesting.[24] Earlier syntheses of Genesis with Greek philosophical concepts had, following Philo, tended to associate woman's inferior origins and subordination with her lesser rationality. Augustine strongly opposed such interpretations, seeing them as inconsistent with Christian commitment to spiritual equality, which he provided with content in terms of Greek ideals of Reason. Augustine also opposed any interpretation of the separate creation of woman which would detract from God's serious purpose in creating sexual difference, as if woman's very existence symbolized the Fall. His own interpretation of the sexual symbolism of Genesis is clearly supposed to defend woman against what he perceived as the misogynism of earlier exegesis. But despite this conscious upgrading of female nature, his own interpretations still put women in an ambivalent position with respect to Reason.

Although the existence of the female sex is no corruption, but natural, male–female relations can none the less, Augustine thought, be appropriately taken as symbolizing relations of proper subordination and dominance within human nature; he devotes much attention to finding a content for woman's subordinate position and helpmate role which does not locate her outside sovereign Reason. There is more at stake here than a quaint preoccupation with getting the right interpretation of Genesis. Within the traditional framework of synthesis of biblical texts and Greek philosophical concepts, Augustine attempted to articulate sexual equality with respect to Reason, while yet finding interpretative content for the Genesis subordination of woman to man. What woman *is* as a rational spirit must, he insists, be distinguished from what she symbolizes in her bodily difference from man. It is this bodily difference that must bear the symbolic weight; and its symbolic role must be articulated without detriment to woman's equality to man in respect of Reason. In the *Confessions*, Augustine tries to meet the challenge by saying that rational man, made in the image and likeness of God, rules over the irrational animals. And just as in man's soul there are two forces – one which 'rules by virtue of the act of deliberation', and another which is 'made subject so that it may obey' – so also, corporeally, woman was made for man. She had:

> a nature equal in mental capacity of rational intelligence, but made subject, by virtue of the sex of her body, to the male sex in the same way that the appetite for action is made subject, in order to conceive by the rational mind the skill of acting rightly.[25]

In respect of her rational intelligence, woman, like man, is subject to God alone. But her bodily difference from man, and the physical subjection which Augustine seems to see as inseparable from it, symbolically represent a subordination relation between two aspects of Reason. Augustine gives a fuller account of their difference in the *De Trinitate*. Woman's physical subordination to man symbolizes the rightful subordination of the mind's practical functions – its control over temporal things, managing the affairs of life – to its higher function in contemplating eternal things. The Genesis story of a helper for man having to be 'taken from himself and formed into his consort' symbolizes the diversion of Reason into practical affairs.

> Just as in man and woman there is one flesh of two, so the one nature of the mind embraces our intellect and action, or our council and execution, or our reason and reasonable appetite, or whatever more significant terms there may be for expressing them, so that as it was said of these: 'Two in one mind'.[26]

This symbolic association with the lesser, practical function of mind is not at all supposed to mean that woman does not possess that higher contemplative function of Reason in virtue of which human beings are made in the image of God. According to Genesis, 'human nature itself, which is complete in both sexes, has been made in the image of God'. None the less, there is a dimension to this image which is sexually differentiated. Man 'by himself alone' is the image of God, just as fully and completely as when he and the woman are joined together into one. Whereas woman, in so far as she is assigned as a helpmate, can be said to be the image of God only together with her husband. This is Augustine's rendering of Paul's injunction (1 Cor. 11: 7, 5) that man, as the image and glory of God, ought not to cover his head; whereas the woman, as the glory of the man, ought to have her head covered.[27] It would be inaccurate here to represent Augustine as claiming that it is only in so far as she is considered in relation to man, whose helpmate she is, that woman can be said to be 'made in God's image', whereas man is thus made in his own right. Augustine's point is, rather, that it is only in so far as woman is considered in her 'helpmate' role that she is *not* in God's image. Woman is rightly said to be not made in the image of God, only in so far as she is the symbol of the mind's direction to practical affairs.

There is, again, much more at stake in all this than a zealous concern with the precise interpretation of a biblical injunction. In these passages, Augustine attempted to make a clear separation between claims about female nature and the role of woman as symbol; to combat any suggestion that women are excluded from the 'renewal in Christ', which is for him a reinforcement of that wherein human beings are made in God's image – Reason. This, he insisted, is located in the spirit or mind, 'where there is no sex'. And woman's role as symbol of mind's diversion into the temporal in no way means that she is incapable of the higher, contemplative form of Reason.

> But because she differs from man by her bodily sex, that part of the reason which is turned aside to regulate temporal things, could be properly symbolised by her corporeal veil; so that the image of God does not remain except in that part of the mind of man in which it clings to the contemplation and consideration of the eternal reasons, which, as is evident, not only men but also women possess.[28]

In all this, Augustine displayed much more sensitivity than Philo to the difference between allegory and the actual character traits of men and women. But, despite his good intentions, his own symbolism pulls against his explicit doctrine of sexual equality with respect to the possession of Reason. Against the background of earlier associations between femininity and inferior aspects of human nature, his symbolic relocation of the feminine can be seen as an upgrading. It is, he insists, only in respect of her bodily difference from man that woman is an appropriate symbol of lesser intellectual functioning; and this, in his philosophy, is a comparatively insignificant difference. What really matters is her status as rational mind, where she is equal to man. But from our perspective it can of course be pointed out that mere bodily difference surely makes the female no more appropriate than the male to the symbolic representation of 'lesser' intellectual functions. What is operating here, again, is the conceptual alignment of maleness with superiority, femaleness with inferiority. Despite his professed commitment to spiritual equality, Augustine's symbolism leaves femininity precariously placed in relation to Reason – close to the sensory entanglements with which Reason must contend in its diversion from superior contemplation. And he elaborates this aspect of the symbols in terms of the corruption of the will through its dealings with sense, thus reinforcing older associations between femaleness and weak-mindedness.

For Augustine, rational mind by right controls external things; but it can instead be drawn into them in excessive love. This was his version of the Fall; and it remained symbolically associated with woman, although it was now presented as a malfunctioning of Reason itself, rather than the subjection of Reason to an alien, intruding sense-perception. The mind's dealings with temporal things can lead it to 'slip ahead too far' in an 'uncontrolled progress':

> and if its head gives its consent, that is, if that which presides as the masculine part in the watch tower of counsel, does not check and restrain it, then it grows old among its enemies, namely the devils with the prince of devils, who are envious of virtue; and that vision of eternal things is likewise withdrawn from the head itself, which in company with its spouse eats what is forbidden, so that the light of its eyes is not with it.[29]

It is true that the mind's practical diversion, symbolized by woman, is not for Augustine a descent into a realm which is alien to Reason. But this application of Reason has 'appetite' very near to it, and is hence vulnerable to corruption. The capacity to form images of material things is essential to the mind's functioning in the material world. And it can readily bind itself excessively to these with the 'glue of love'.[30] Augustine saw this defiling 'fornication of the phantasy' as a defect of the will. And the surrender of the will in such entanglements remained for him symbolically associated with woman. This is an aspect of a wider symbolic association between women and passion – with the 'carnalization of the mind' which is the consequence of the will's loss of control. For Augustine, it is this loss of control which makes bodily lust so disturbing; for it is out of keeping with the body's rightful subjection to mind. Such 'contention, fight and altercation' of lust and will is the consequence of man's original sin of disobedience. Without it, the 'organ of generation' would have obeyed the will, as do other bodily organs, sowing seed in 'the field of birth' as the hand sows seed in the 'field of earth'.[31] Woman, as the object of male lust, is associated with this distressing subjection of mind to body.

Augustine replaced the older sexual symbolism in deference to spiritual equality, but structurally the situation is much the same as before. It is by resisting being dragged down into the will's entanglements with fornications of phantasy, still associated with woman, that the soul pursues the life of Reason and virtue. Woman remains associated with bodily perturbation, in opposition to Reason. And her 'natural' subordination to man represents rational control, the subjection of flesh to spirit in the right ordering of things.[32] The life of Reason, Augustine insisted, is open to woman as the spiritual equal of man. But it remained the case that the male, in pursuing the life of Reason, need deny only those aspects of human nature which are already external to his symbolic being. Woman, despite her status as co-heir of grace, must pursue that same path burdened by the symbolic force of her subordination to man, which Augustine saw as natural.

Aquinas: 'the principle of the human race' and his 'helpmate'

Augustine's utilization of Greek thought drew mainly on Plato. In the thirteenth century, his own thought – with the Platonic overtones somewhat played down – occurred, alongside that of Aristotle, as an 'authority' in the most famous of all the attempted syntheses of Greek and Christian thought – the *Summa Theologica* of St Thomas Aquinas. From Aristotle, Aquinas derived a more integrated view of human nature than was typical of the more Platonic spirit of Augustine. Augustine had stressed the soul's unity amidst the diversity of its operations. But an array of Aristotelian distinctions between 'actualities' and 'potentialities', 'powers' and 'functions', 'subjects' and 'principles', allowed Aquinas a much more precise articulation of this theme. The soul is a unity, despite its different powers; and the power which is the mind is a unity, despite its different functions.

Another dimension of the soul's unity in Aquinas's philosophy came from his development of the Aristotelian notion of substantial form as the intelligible principle of a body. The intellectual soul is the form of a living human body. This soul has intellect as one of its powers; but it is also the principle of the lesser, non-intellectual processes involved in being human. In non-rational animals, these sensitive or vegetative processes have as their principle inferior, non-intellectual souls. But the intellectual soul contains 'virtually' within it the less perfect forms, to which are ascribed the less noble, non-intellectual functions of human nature.[33] Being but one thing, the living human being has but one substantial form – the intellectual soul – but that soul is the principle not just of intellect, but also of the lesser functions. This does not mean, however, that it is in all cases their 'subject'. The intellectual soul is the principle of sense, as well as of understanding and will. But only understanding and will are properly said to be *in* it as their subject. Sensation is present not in the soul, but rather in the human composite of soul and body; although it is *by* the intellectual soul that the composite has the power of sense.

With this comparatively sophisticated apparatus for handling the theme of the soul's unity amidst diversity, it is not surprising that Aquinas should have found no use for male–female symbolism as an expression of a division between parts or elements of the soul, or of the intrusions of sense into mind. None the less, his account of human nature yields yet another rendering of the Genesis story of male–female relations.

Aquinas's interpretation of the Genesis story makes use of the concept of *principle* as that from which operations flow – that in which they have their intelligible rationale: 'as God is the principle of the whole universe, so the first man, in likeness to God, was the principle of the whole human race.'[34] And this provides a sense in which man, but not woman, is made in the image of God. Citing Augustine as authority, Aquinas insists that intellectual nature – the image of God in its principal signification – is found in both men and women; it is in the mind, 'wherein there is no sexual distinction'. But in a secondary sense it is found in man, but not in woman, 'for man is the beginning and end of woman; as God is the beginning and end of every creature'. Man was not created for woman, but woman for man.[35]

This secondary sense, in which woman, not being the principle of the race, is not made in God's image, is spelled out by Aquinas in terms of a distinction between human 'vital functioning' as against 'generation'. There is among all animals a vital operation – nobler than generation – to which their life is principally directed. And in the case of man this vital function which provides the direction of life involves something still nobler – intellectual operation. Because human vital functioning, unlike that of the animals, includes this noble intellectual aspect, there is in this case, he thinks, a greater reason for the distinction between vital functioning and generation. For Aquinas, it is this distinction that is symbolized by the Genesis story of the separate creation of woman. The first man symbolizes human vital functioning, including Reason; he is the principle of the race, that in which its nature can be identified. Woman, separately created, symbolizes generation – the perpetuation of that nature summed up in man. It is her role in generation, Aquinas suggests, that makes her man's helpmate. In areas of life other than generation, 'man can be more efficiently helped by another man'.[36]

For Aquinas, then, woman does not symbolize an inferior form or lesser presence of rationality. But her meaning is bound up with the reproduction of human nature, in distinction from those operations – including noble intellectual functioning – which define what human nature *is*. Despite Aquinas's insistence that she is 'made in God's image' in respect of the 'rational principle', she is symbolically located outside the actual manifestations of Reason within human life. And despite his insistence that the subordination of woman in Genesis should not be taken as symbolizing her lesser rationality, there are many indications in the *Summa Theologica* that this is not because he believed that women were as rational as men. The inferior and subordinate being of woman does not, as some of Aquinas's opponents would have it, mean that her very existence is to be attributed to the corrupting effects of the Fall, rather than to the original state of creation. But, like Augustine, Aquinas is committed not only to the naturalness of woman's existence, but also to that of her subordination; and he sees it as grounded in the predominance of Reason in the male: 'good order would have been wanting in the human family if some were not governed by others wiser than themselves. So by such a kind of subjection woman is naturally subject to man, because in man, the discretion of reason predominates.'[37]

Aquinas, in a later section of the *Summa Theologica*, cites with approval Aristotle's assertion that women are not properly describable as 'continent', because they are 'vacillating' through being unstable of reason, and are easily led, so that they follow their passions readily.[38] And he groups women with children and imbeciles as unable to give reliable evidence on grounds of a 'defect in reason'.[39] His acceptance of the Aristotelian doctrine of generation means, too, that even in reproduction, of which she is the appropriate symbol, woman plays only an ancillary passive role, and her own generation is defective. The active force in the male seed, he says, echoing Aristotle,

tends to the production of a perfect likeness in the masculine sex; while the production of woman comes from defect in the active force or from some material indisposition, or even from some external influence; such as that of a south wind, which is moist, as the Philosopher observes.[40]

Aquinas repudiated interpretations of Genesis which treated woman as a symbol of lesser possession or lesser forms of Reason. But her new symbolic location, associated merely with the reproduction of a human nature outside her, serves to reinforce her symbolic exclusion from the actual manifestations of Reason. And the influence of Aristotle in Aquinas's thought gives new strength to the idea of the actual inferiority of female Reason.

These early versions of woman's relations to Reason presented her, in some manner or other, as derivative in relation to a male paradigm of rational excellence – as an addition to and, despite her helpmate role, often as an encumbrance to an essentially male humanity. It should by now be clear that more is at stake in all this than the niceties of biblical exegesis; and more, too, than a succession of surface misogynist attitudes within philosophical thought. The 'male bias', if we can call it that, of past philosophical thought about Reason goes deeper than that. It is not a question simply of the applicability to women of neutrally specified ideals of rationality, but rather of the genderization of the ideals themselves. An exclusion or transcending of the feminine is built into past ideals of Reason as the sovereign human character trait. And correlatively, as we shall see in later chapters, the content of femininity has been partly formed by such processes of exclusion.

3
Reason as attainment

Introduction

In *The Philosophy of Right*, Hegel contrasted the 'happy ideas, taste and elegance' characteristic of female consciousness with male attainments which demand a 'universal faculty'. 'Women are educated – who knows how? – as it were by breathing in ideas, by living rather than by acquiring knowledge. The status of manhood, on the other hand, is attained only by the stress of thought and much technical exertion.'[1] These kinds of connection between maleness and achievement are not confined to Hegel. In western thought, maleness has been seen as itself an achievement, attained by breaking away from the more 'natural' condition of women. Attitudes to Reason and its bearing on the rest of life have played a major part in this; a development that occurred in the seventeenth century has been particularly crucial.

In the illustrations, in the last chapter, of Reason's superiority over other aspects of human nature, it was seen as a distinctive human trait, with ramifications in all areas of life – the practical, no less than the contemplative – even if, as with Augustine, this was regarded as an inferior diversion of Reason. In the seventeenth century, Reason came to be seen not just as a distinguishing feature of human nature, but as an achievement – a skill to be learned, a distinctively methodical way of thinking, sharply differentiated from other kinds of thought – and its relationships with other aspects of human nature were also transformed. The most thoroughgoing and influential version of Reason as methodical thought was the famous method of Descartes. Something happened here which proved crucial for the development of stereotypes of maleness and femaleness, and it happened in some ways despite Descartes's explicit intentions.

Descartes's method

In its Greek origins, the basic meaning of 'method' was a road or path to be followed; and the metaphor of a path whose goal is understanding recurs throughout the entire philosophical tradition which grew from Greek thought. The method which proceeds without analysis, says Socrates in Plato's *Phaedrus*, is 'like the groping of a blind man'.[2] The follower of true method is preserved from such blind wandering by understanding the reason for which things are done in a certain order. Descartes used the same metaphors. In expounding his 'rules for the direction of the mind', he attacked those truth-seekers who 'conduct their minds along unexplored routes, having no reason to hope for success, but merely being willing to risk the experiment of finding whether the truth they seek lies there'. It is, he says, as if a man seeking treasure

were to 'continuously roam the streets, seeking to find
something that a passer-by might have chanced to drop'.[3]
But, although his description of the goal remained much the
same, Descartes completely transformed the relationship
between Reason and method which had been central in the
intellectual tradition since the time of Socrates.

The original Socratic ideal of method, illustrated by the
definition of love, is expounded in the concluding sections of
the *Phaedrus*. Right method, says Socrates, involves processes
of generalization, the 'survey of scattered particulars, leading
to their comprehension in one idea'; and processes of division
into species, 'according to the natural formation, where the
joint is, not breaking any part as a bad carver might'. These
processes are aids to speaking and thinking; they belong in
the art of rhetoric. But they are also supposed to be guides to
truth, helping those who practise them to discern a 'one and
many' in Nature. Most of the ingredients for later developments in the idea of method can be found in these brief
Phaedrus passages: the idea of an orderly procedure; of an
analysis to be conducted in relation to an end to be achieved;
the connections between method and teaching; the importance of understanding the nature of the soul, in which
persuasion is supposed to be induced. The ability to impart
the Socratic art of rhetoric involves grasping its nature and
relating its parts to the end which is supposed to be achieved
in the soul. However, Socrates' general description of the art
of rhetoric passed into the tradition as a general rubric which
could be extended to any art: the teacher must have an
understanding of what the art deals with and be able to
analyse and evaluate its parts in relation to the achievement
of its end.

Aristotle developed the idea of a systematic treatment of
the art of arguing and debating into a concern with a rational
way – a reasoned procedure – for arriving at sound
conclusions. But the relation of reason to the 'way' or
'method' was similar to the original Socratic version. Reason
– whether applied to the art of persuasion, to other arts, or

more narrowly to the investigations which are supposed to yield truth – was incorporated into method. Method was a reasoned way of pursuing an activity; and it was the grasp of this internal reason which was supposed to enable the activity to be taught.

In Descartes's system, in contrast, method became not so much a reasoned way of proceeding – a path to be followed rationally – as a way of reaso*ning*: a precisely ordered mode of abstract thinking. And the right order of thought was to be determined not by the variable subject-matter and ends of the activities at issue, but by the natural operations of the mind itself. Descartes's actual definitions of method are on the surface not very different from earlier ideas of method. By a method, he says in his *Rules for the Direction of the Mind*, he means 'certain and simple rules such that, if a man observe them accurately, he shall never assume what is false as true, and will never spend his mental efforts to no purpose, but will always gradually increase his knowledge and so arrive at a true understanding of all that does not surpass his powers'.[4] To see what is really distinctive and important about Descartes's method we must see it in the context of the metaphysical doctrine for which he is most notorious – the radical separateness of mind and body – and also in the context of his immediate predecessors in the development of ideas of method.

Descartes's method, he insisted, is unitary and yields truth regardless of subject-matter. He criticized his Aristotelian scholastic predecessors for holding that the certainty of mathematics was unattainable in other sciences and that the method of each science should vary with differences in the material it investigated. A single and identical method, he thought, could be applied to all the various sciences, for the sciences taken together were nothing else but the very unity of human reason itself. This vision of the unity of the sciences as reflecting that of Reason arose directly from Descartes's radical separation of mind and body. Where body is involved, the formation of one habit inhibits that of others. The hand that adapts itself to agricultural operations is thereby less likely to be adept at harp playing. But the sciences consist entirely in the cognitive exercise of the mind. The traditional conception of a multiplicity of methods for different subject-areas thus rests on a faulty assimilation of mind to body. The sciences do not share in the inevitable multiplicity of the bodily arts. Knowing one truth does not have the restricting effect that is the consequence of mastering a bodily art; in fact it aids us in finding out other truths. So the sciences, taken all together, are identical with human wisdom, which always remains one and the same, however applied to different subjects.[5]

All this is strongly opposed to what Descartes saw as the arbitrariness of the prevailing scholastic curriculum divisions. This concern was not new. Descartes's humanist predecessors had also been dissatisfied with the arbitrary methods of presentation of the traditional disciplines which, they thought, created needless difficulties for students. In the sixteenth century, Peter Ramus had devised 'one simple method' to bring order into the subjects taught in universities. Ramus's method proceeded from universal and general principles down to the more specific and singular, an order which he supposed to reflect the different degrees of clarity among the parts of a discipline. The clearer was to precede the more obscure, following the order and progression from universal to singular. Aristotle had distinguished what is prior in nature and what is prior to us. Ramus's ideal was a right order and progression of thought, which would reflect the priority in nature of the universal over the particular. But there was no real justification for his conviction that what was prior in being should also be clearer to students.[6]

For Descartes, the idea of a right order of thought was grounded in an understanding of the nature of the mind. The correspondence between the basic structures of human thought and the order of the world, he argued, is divinely guaranteed. To find and to follow the mind's most basic operations was for him not just a prerequisite for ease in learning. His organization of subject-matter in accordance with what is more apparent to an attentive mind was not just a pedagogical device. Clarity and distinctness were the marks of truth. His method was directed to uncovering those basic ideas whose truth was assured by the fact that a veracious God created both the mind and the material world. Method was not confined to pedagogy; it was linked with criteria of truth.

As a development in the politics of learning, the significance of this approach to method cannot be overestimated. Earlier Renaissance reforms of educational procedures often found themselves in conflict with those who saw following the 'natural' processes of the mind as less important than following approved methods of strict demonstration and proof, however difficult these may have been to impart to students. Descartes's method undercut this conflict. Its aim went beyond the transmission of an already established art or the successful pursuit of a course of study; it aimed at valid knowledge. It should not be seen, he insisted, as a means of persuasion, belonging in the art of rhetoric; it belonged, rather, with the discovery of new truth. But such discovery was assured precisely through following the natural processes of thought. At the same time, Descartes's grounding of this unified method in the unity of Reason itself, accessible through introspection, enabled him to separate method entirely from the realm of public pedagogy and disputation.

The implications for Reason of thus severing the links between method and public procedures of discourse, debate and successful argument were far reaching. The right ordering of ideas was no longer associated with the best arrangement of the school curricula, but with private abstract thought, which can be pursued quite independently of public educational structures and procedures. Persuasion was internalized as what is clear and apparent to an attentive mind – the mark of truth itself. Reasoning in accordance with this new method does not demand conformity with the subtle forms of argument accepted as valid in the public disputations of the schools. The emphasis is entirely on unaided Reason. Descartes presented the method as simply a systematization of the innate faculty of Reason or 'good sense' – the power of 'forming good judgement and of distinguishing the true from the false'. And this natural light of Reason is supposedly equal in all.[7]

Descartes saw his method as opening the way to a new egalitarianism in knowledge. In a letter written shortly after the publication of the *Discourse on Method*, he commented that his thoughts on method seemed to him appropriate to put in a book where he wished that 'even women' might understand something.[8] From our perspective, this tone may sound patronizing, but the remark is to be understood against the background of associations between earlier Renaissance versions of method and pedagogical procedures. By and large, it was only boys who were given systematic formal education outside the home. The exclusion of women from method was a direct consequence of their exclusion from the schools in which it was pursued. Descartes's egalitarian intentions come out also in his insistence on writing the *Discourse on Method* in the vernacular, rather than in Latin, the learned language of the schools. The work, he stressed, should appeal to those who avail themselves only of their natural reason in its purity.[9] The point was political as well as practical. The use of Latin was in many ways the distinguishing mark of the learned. Women, being educated mostly at home rather than in the schools, had no direct access to the learned, Latin-speaking world. The teaching of Latin to boys thus marked the boundaries between the private world of the family, in which the vernacular was used, and the external world of learning, to which males had access.[10] The accessibility of the new method even to women was thus a powerful symbol of the transformation which it marked in the relationship between method and autonomous, individual reasoning.

In place of the subtleties of scholastic disputation, which can only, he thought, obscure the mind's natural clarity, Descartes offered a few supposedly simple procedures, the rationale of which was to remove all obstacles to the natural operations of the mind. The general rubric of the method was to break down the more complex operations of the mind into their simplest forms and then recombine them in an orderly series. The complex and obscure is reduced to simple, self-evident 'intuitions', which the mind scrutinizes with 'steadfast, mental gaze', then combines in orderly chains of deductions.[11] Anyone who follows this method can feel assured that 'no avenue to the truth is closed to him from which everyone else is not also excluded, and that his ignorance is due neither to a deficiency in his capacity nor to his method of procedure'.[12]

Descartes's method, with its new emphasis on the privacy of the mind's natural operations, promised to make knowledge accessible to all, even to women. Such was his intent. The lasting influence of his method, however, was something quite different, though no less a product of his radical separation of mind and body. In the context of associations already existing between gender and Reason, his version of the mind–body relationship produced stark polarizations of previously existing contrasts. This came about not through any intellectual move made within his system, but as a by-product of his transformation of the relations between Reason and its opposites. Descartes strongly repudiated his medieval predecessors' idea of a divided soul, which had Reason – identified with the authentic character of a human being – struggling with lesser parts of the soul. For him, the soul was not to be divided into higher (intellectual) and lower (sensitive) parts; it was an indivisible unity, identified with pure intellect. He replaced the medieval philosophers' divisions between higher and lower parts of the soul with the dichotomy between mind and body. In this limited respect, Descartes's system echoed the thought of the early Plato. In place of the older divisions within the soul he introduced a division between the soul – now identified again with the mind – and body; the non-rational was no longer part of the soul, but pertained entirely to body.

There is within us but one soul, and this soul has not in itself any diversity of parts; the same part that is subject to sense impressions is rational, and all the soul's appetites are acts of will. The error which has been committed in making it play the part of various personages, usually in opposition one to another, only proceeds from the fact that we have not properly distinguished its functions from those of the body, to which alone we must attribute everything which can be observed in us that is opposed to our reason.[13]

The drama of dominance between human traits persisted in Descartes's philosophy, but it was played out as a struggle between the soul itself – equated with pure intellect – and body. He saw the encroachments of non-intellectual passion, sense or imagination as coming not from lower parts or aspects of the soul, but from altogether outside the soul – as intrusions from body. Descartes's method is founded on this alignment between the bodily and the non-rational. It involves forming the habit of distinguishing intellectual from corporeal matters. And this search for the purely intellectual – the clear and distinct – made possible polarizations of previously existing contrasts, which had previously been drawn within the boundaries of the soul. Those aspects of human nature which Reason must dominate had not previously been so sharply delineated from the intellectual. The distinction between Reason and its opposites could now coincide with Descartes's very sharp distinction – than which, as he says, none can be sharper – between mind and body.

Descartes's alignment between the Reason–non-Reason and mind–body distinctions brought with it the notion of a distinctive kind of rational thought as a highly restricted activity. Augustine had presented the mind's dealings with practical matters as a diversion of a unitary Reason from its superior function of contemplation. This diversion was at risk of entanglement with sense, but it was not thereby different in kind from the Reason employed in contemplative thought. Descartes separated thought of the kind that yields certainty much more sharply from the practical concerns of life. It was for him a highly rarefied exercise of intellect, a complete transcending of the sensuous – a highly arduous activity which cannot be expected to occupy more than a very small part of a normal life. In the *Discourse on Method*, he stressed the contrasts between the demands of enquiry into truth and the attitudes appropriate to the practical activities of life. The foundations of the enquiry into truth demand that the mind rigorously enact the metaphysical truth of its separateness from body. This securing of the foundations of knowledge is a separate activity from the much more relaxed pursuits of everyday life, where mind must accept its intermingling with body. Descartes's separation of mind and body yielded a vision of a unitary pure thought, ranging like the common light of the sun over a variety of objects. Its unitariness, however, served also to separate it from the rest of life.

Pure thought of this rarefied kind secures the foundations of science. However, most of scientific activity itself involves exercise of the imagination rather than of pure intellect; scientific investigation, although it demands sustained effort and training, occupies an intermediate position between pure intellect and the confusion of sense. The rest of life is rightly given over to the sway of the senses, to that muddled zone of confused perception where mind and body intermingle. In his correspondence with Princess Elizabeth, Descartes again stressed that arduous clear and distinct thought, of the kind that secures the foundations of science, can and should occupy only a small part of a well-spent life. If we can take seriously his autobiographical remarks to her – as he insists she should – it is something to which he himself devoted only a few hours a year.[14] It is through pure intellect, transcending the intrusion of body, that we grasp the separateness of mind and body on which true science is founded. The greater part of the life of a Cartesian self is lived in the zone of confused, sensuous awareness. However, it is sustained there by the metaphysical truth, which pure thought can grasp, of the absolute separateness of mind and body; and by the possibility of a complete science grounded in this truth. Underlying the confusion of the senses, there is a crystalline realm of order, where sharply articulated structures of thought perfectly match the structure of intelligible reality. These clear, matching structures of mind and matter underlie the confused realm of the sensuous produced by the intermingling of both. Individual minds can rest assured that there is an underlying right order of thought, which provides a secure underpinning for lives lived predominantly in the realm of the sensuous; the confusions of sense and imagination hold no ultimate threat.

Arduous as the grasp of the metaphysical basis of Descartes's method may be, the method itself was supposed to be accessible to all. And within the terms of the system there is, in all this, no differentiation between male and female minds. Both must be seen as equally intellectual substances, endowed with good sense or Reason. The difference in intellectual achievement between men and women, no less than that between different men, must arise not from some being more rational than others, but 'solely from the fact that our thoughts pass through diverse channels and the same objects are not considered by all'.[15] But removing method from the restraints of public pedagogy did not, in practice, make knowledge any more accessible to women. Descartes's method may be essentially private and accessible to all. But for him, no less than Bacon, the new science was, none the less, a collective endeavour. It is by 'joining together the lives and labours of many', he says in the concluding section of the *Discourse on Method*, that science will progress.[16] It is through a corporate exercise, however non-corporeal may be its ultimate metaphysical foundation, that the new science will advance, rendering humanity the promised goal of becoming 'masters and possessors of nature'.[17] Descartes thought his account of the mind opened the way to a newly egalitarian pursuit of knowledge. But the channels through which those basically equal resources of Reason had to flow remained more convoluted, even for noble women, than for men. Elizabeth poignantly expressed the situation in one of her letters to Descartes:

the life I am constrained to lead does not allow me enough free time to acquire a habit of meditation in accordance with your rules. Sometimes the interests of my household, which I must not neglect, sometimes conversations and civilities I cannot eschew, so throughly deject this weak mind with annoyances or boredom that it remains, for a long time afterward, useless for anything else.[18]

The realities of the lives of women, despite their supposed equality in Reason, precluded them, too, from any significant involvement in the collective endeavours of science, the developing forms of which quickly outstripped the private procedures of Descartes's method.

It is not just impinging social realities, however, which militate against sexual equality in this new version of Reason's relations with science. There are aspects of Descartes's thought which – however unintentionally – provided a basis for a sexual division of mental labour whose influence is still very much with us. Descartes's emphasis on the equality of Reason had less influence than his formative contribution to the ideal of a distinctive kind of Reason – a highly abstract mode of thought, separable, in principle, from the emotional complexities and practical demands of ordinary life. This was not the only kind of thought which Descartes recognized as rational. In the Sixth Meditation he acknowledged that the inferior senses, once they have been set aside from the search for truth – where they can only mislead and distort – are reliable guides to our well-being. To trust them is not irrational. He does not maintain that we are rational only when exercising arduous pure thought, engaged in intellectual contemplation and assembling chains of deduction. Indeed, he thinks it is not rational to spend an excessive amount of time in such purely intellectual activity.[19] None the less, through his philosophy, Reason took on special associations with the realm of pure thought, which provides the foundations of science, and with the deductive ratiocination which was of the essence of his method. And the sharpness of his separation of the ultimate requirements of truth-seeking from the practical affairs of everyday life reinforced already existing distinctions between male and female roles, opening the way to the idea of distinctive male and female consciousness.

We owe to Descartes an influential and pervasive theory of mind, which provides support for a powerful version of the sexual division of mental labour. Women have been assigned responsibility for that realm of the sensuous which the Cartesian Man of Reason must transcend, if he is to have true knowledge of things. He must move on to the exercise of disciplined imagination, in most of scientific activity; and to the rigours of pure intellect, if he would grasp the ultimate foundations of science. Woman's task is to preserve the sphere of the intermingling of mind and body, to which the Man of Reason will repair for solace, warmth and relaxation. If he is to exercise the most exalted form of Reason, he must leave soft emotions and sensuousness behind; woman will keep them intact for him. The way was thus opened for women to be associated with not just a lesser presence of Reason, but a different kind of intellectual character, construed as complementary to 'male' Reason. This crucial development springs from the accentuation of women's exclusion from Reason, now conceived – in its highest form – as an attainment.

Hume on Reason and the passions

Descartes's method transformed Reason into a uniform, undifferentiated skill, abstracted from any determinate subject-matter. This loss of differentiation gave rise to another crucial change: Reason lost the strong motivational force it had in earlier thought. In the lack of inner direction to specific ends, Descartes's Reason became an inert instrument, needing direction by an extraneous will. For him, the understanding lacked even the power to affirm or deny, and its polarization from the non-rational bodily passions deprived it also of the capacity to struggle directly with non-rational forces. Plato's Reason, in contrast, was presented as straining of its own resources towards truth; and in the 'divided-soul' model, Reason deliberated about ends, decided between them and struggled with the passions to determine which end would prevail. Aristotle, too, despite his repudiation of the divided soul, presented Reason as controlling or subduing by its own force the emotional part of human nature.

For Descartes, Reason's origins ensured it a connection with truth and with human well-being, though one that depended on an extraneous divine benevolence. But if his supporting theological views are repudiated, the impotence of this methodical abstract thought becomes apparent. Spinoza, reacting against the passivity of Descartes's version of Reason, rejected the distinction between will and understanding, making Reason an active, emotional force, able – like the earlier Greek versions of Reason – to engage with passions in its own right. But it was Descartes's version of Reason that prevailed; and its inherent inertness and impotence appeared most starkly in Hume's version of Reason. For Hume, Reason has of itself no power to control passion or to deliberate about ends. Its motivating force lies always outside itself, in the driving force of passion. Under the aegis of different passions, it is directed to different ends. Reason has of itself no power to deliberate about ends or to choose between them; and it entirely lacks the affective force necessary to struggle with the passions. It 'is and ought to be nothing but the slave of the passions, pretending to no other office but to serve and obey them.'[20]

What are the implications of this reversal for the male–female distinction? We might expect it to loosen the alignment between maleness and Reason, but what actually happens is a subtle reinforcement of the older pattern. To see how this is so we must look more closely at Hume's restructuring of the Reason–passion distinction, and at its repercussions in Kant's treatment of the role of Reason in morality.

Hume turned on its head the seventeenth-century rational-ists' picture of the role of Reason in knowledge and, more generally, in human life. For him, all our beliefs about the world, all our knowledge of matters of fact, resolve into expectations of stability, predictability and constancy arising from customary associations in the mind. Reason plays no part in all this; belief is a function of our sensitive rather than of our cognitive nature. Reason can conjoin ideas in chains of necessary deduction; but these cannot yield understanding of the real natures of things. Reason yields knowledge in strictly limited areas of thought, such as logic and mathematics, where all that is involved is a grasp of entirely formal relations between ideas; knowledge of 'matters of fact', however, is the province not of Reason, but of imagination. The understanding which delivers the world to us is reduced to 'the general and more established properties of the imagination', in contrast to the 'trivial suggestions of the fancy'.[21] Its reliability rests entirely on the force of our 'strong propensities', under the force of Custom, to consider things in a certain way. For Descartes, conformity to Reason determined what is or is not to be regarded as 'natural'; for Hume, it was the other way round: Reason must rest on and conform to our natural propensities. 'Where reason is lively, and mixes itself with some propensity, it ought to be assented to. Where it does not, it never can have any title to operate upon us.'[22] These strong inclinations are the test of what is trustworthy in human thought, and provide the motivating force for a Reason which is of itself entirely inert.

A new and, at first sight, disconcerting picture emerges of the role of Reason in morality. Reason can still discover connections between things, but it has no role in how those connections affect us. Of itself it can never 'produce any action or give rise to volition'. Nor can it prevent volition, or 'dispute the preference' with any passion or emotion.[23] The supposed pre-eminence of Reason above passion rests on a misunderstanding; the principle which opposes our passion is called reason only in an improper sense. Hume's argument for this conclusion is not altogether persuasive. Passions, he points out, are not susceptible of agreement or disagreement with relations of ideas or matters of fact, and are therefore incapable of being true or false – a prerequisite for being in conflict with Reason. But what is important here is not Hume's justification of the point, but its import for his understanding of morals.

> Where a passion is neither founded on false suppositions, nor chuses means insufficient for the ends, the understanding can neither justify nor condemn it. 'Tis not contrary to reason to prefer the destruction of the whole world to the scratching of my finger. 'Tis not contrary to reason for me to chuse my total ruin, to prevent the least uneasiness of an Indian or person wholly unknown to me. 'Tis as little contrary to reason to prefer even my own acknowledg'd lesser good to my greater, and have a more ardent affection for the former than the latter.[24]

Hume's point is not that any of these stances should be regarded as acceptable to people of good sense, but rather that their being or not being so is in no way a matter of Reason. Moral distinctions are not the 'offspring of reason', which is wholly inactive.[25] They derive from a moral sense grounded in feelings or sentiment. Hume acknowledged that the idea that moral distinctions derive from passions, in relation to which Reason is utterly impotent, would meet with resistance. But he diagnosed this resistance as resulting from conflating with Reason what are in fact 'calm passions' – actions of the mind which resemble Reason in that they operate with the same calmness and tranquillity, producing little emotion in the mind. Such calm passions as benevolence and resentment, the love of life, kindness to children or 'the general appetite to good, and aversion to evil' influence the mind no less than the more violent passions of resentment, fear or apprehension. What we call 'strength of mind' implies the prevalence of the calm passions above the violent; and this, Hume suggests, is what is 'vulgarly' called reason. It refers to affections of the same kind as the passions, but 'such as operate more calmly, and cause no disorder in the temper'. But their comparative tranquillity causes us to regard them as conclusions only of our intellectual faculties. Generally speaking, it is the violent passions that have the more powerful influence on the will. But it is often found that the calm ones, 'when corroborated by reflection, and seconded by resolution', are 'able to controul them in their most furious movements'. This 'struggle of passion and reason', as it is called, Hume concludes, 'diversifies human life', making men different 'not only from each other, but also from themselves in different times'.[26]

On the basis of this general distinction between calm and violent passions, Hume reconstructs the distinction between Reason and passion in terms of two forms of acquisitiveness or self-interest; he argues that the curbing of one by the other is the basis of civil society.[27] The more primitive forms of the passion of acquisitiveness produce inevitable conflicts in large societies; for acquisitiveness combines destructively with partiality of affection – the tendency to give priority to our own interests and those of our immediate relatives. The 'first and most natural sentiment of morals' is associated with this immediate prefer- ence for ourselves and friends above strangers. But it combines with the passion of acquisitiveness to produce inevitable social conflict. The resources available to satisfy the passion of acquisitiveness are limited; and the avid desire to acquire goods and possessions for ourselves and our nearest friends is 'insatiable, perpetual, universal and directly destructive of society'. So the 'partial and contradictory motions of the passions of different individuals' must be restrained, if society is to survive.

However, this passion – like all passions, according to Hume – can be controlled only by a stronger one; and the only passion strong enough to regulate and restrain it is acquisitiveness itself. It alone has sufficient force and proper direction to counterbal- ance the love of gain and render men fit members of society by making them abstain from the possessions of others. If it is to play this restraining role, it must first undergo a change of direction. But this readily happens, Hume thinks, on the slightest reflection,

> since 'tis evident, that the passion is much better satisfy'd by its restraint, than by its liberty, and that in preserving

society, we make much greater advances in acquiring possessions, than in the solitary and forlorn condition, which must follow upon violence and an universal licence.[28]

The preservation of society thus rests on the control of acquisitiveness by a more reflective and far-sighted version of itself: 'whether the passion of self-interest be esteemed vicious or virtuous, 'tis all of a case; since itself alone restrains it: So that if it be virtuous, men become social by their virtue; if vicious, their vice has the same effect.'

In this reconstruction of the old theme of the subordination of passion to Reason, control is exercised not strictly by Reason, but by a calm, reflective form of passion – an enlightened self-interest. But the resulting operations of justice in society can be ascribed to Reason in an improper sense, in that they involve considering objects 'at a distance'. From this more detached perspective, preference can be given to 'whatever is in itself preferable' – a principle that is 'often contradictory to those propensities that display themselves upon the approach of the object'.[29]

Reason, as reflective passion, remains for Hume a weak and vulnerable force in comparison with more immediate forms of acquisitiveness. In the normal course of events, it does not prevail over the more intense attractions of objects close by. To have efficacy it must be embodied in externally imposed authority. The social remedy for destructive self-interest depends on making the long-term observance of justice the immediate interest of particular persons who take responsibility for the execution of justice. When the reflective form of acquisitiveness is embodied in institutions of justice, 'men acquire a security against each others' weakness and passion, as well as against their own, and under the shelter of their governors, begin to taste at ease the sweets of society and mutual assistance'.[30]

This, then, is Hume's version of the relationship between Reason and passion: immediate self-interest subjected to the control of a higher and more reflective version of itself. Reason in its 'improper' sense – whether it be 'calm' as against 'violent' passions, 'reflective' as against 'immediate' and 'partial' self-interest, or 'remote' perspective embodied in magistrates as against the pursuit of short-term interests – controls passion. And this relation of dominance or control is articulated in terms of a distinction between 'public' and 'private' interests. The public passion of acquisitiveness is given the role of curbing private interest in acquiring goods and possessions for the sake of the individual and his family.

Hume does not pursue the implications of his reconstruction of the Reason–passion distinction for male–female relations. But the individual whose private interests must be controlled by considerations of justice is perforce, of course, the male head of a household. Women are associated with 'private' passion, because it is on their behalf that male household heads pursue private acquisitiveness. In its social context, Hume's version of Reason, like Descartes's, which made it possible, takes on associations with maleness, even if these are not specifically required by their philosophical theory.

4
Reason and progress

Introduction

For Bacon, the progress of suitably reformed arts and sciences was the basis of humanity's greatest hopes. And Descartes, despite their many differences about knowledge, shared Bacon's vision of the human race becoming, through the advance of science, the masters and possessors of Nature. This optimism about the fruits to be expected from the proliferation of organized knowledge was echoed in the eighteenth century in the manifestos of the Enlightenment, epitomized in Condorcet's vision of the human race 'emancipated from its shackles, released from the empire of fate and from that of the enemies of its progress, advancing with a firm and sure step along the path of truth, virtue and happiness'.[1]

Such exhilaration at the apparently unlimited prospects of human control of Nature through knowledge was not shared by Rousseau. But his repudiation of the Enlightenment vision was accompanied by his own version of the progress of Reason, which interacted in quite different, but equally influential, ways with the male–female distinction. The proper relationship between Reason and Nature was central to Rousseau's treatment of knowledge; and this meant that Reason itself had to be understood in a new way. Rousseau's ideal of Reason was not an abstract scientific knowledge, dominating Nature; but rather Nature, as it were, turned reflective in moral wisdom. For him, Reason was a dynamic development from Nature, not an instrument of external control. Reason emerges from Nature and closeness to Nature is the mark of its authenticity. In this version of the progress of Reason (which was to be further developed by Hegel), Nature lies both in the past, as an object of Reason's backward-looking nostalgia, and in the future, as the goal of Reason's fulfilment. This enabled a new resolution of the ambivalence of the feminine to enter western thought. The feminine was construed as an immature stage of consciousness, left behind by advancing Reason, but also as an object of adulation, as the exemplar for Reason's aspirations to a future return to Nature.

Rousseau: the lost youth of the world

In the midst of general Enlightenment optimism, the voice of Rousseau struck a discordant note. Rousseau admired the great minds of the previous century, but the proliferation and diffusion of knowledge, which his contemporaries hailed as the path to human freedom and happiness, was for him a suspect blessing. It was not so much the ideal of enlightenment through learning that he challenged as the prevailing spirit of optimism about progress through the popularization of knowledge. While admiring those geniuses – Bacon, Descartes, Newton – whom 'nature intended for her disciples', Rousseau thought they should be emulated only by 'those who feel themselves able to walk alone in their footsteps and outstrip them'. Only those few should aspire to 'raise monuments to the glory of the human understanding'.[2] In contrast to Bacon's vision of progress through a burgeoning of the arts and sciences, Rousseau's ideal for the organization of knowledge was that a few 'learned of the first rank' should be given an 'honourable refuge' in the courts of princes, where they might by their influence promote 'the happiness of the people they have enlightened by their wisdom'.[3]

Rousseau's doubts about the ideal of progress through the spread of learning were expressed in the same imagery of an elusive feminized Nature that Bacon used; but its point was quite different. In Rousseau's version, a benevolent Nature hides her secrets from men for their own good.

> Let men learn for once that nature would have preserved them from science, as a mother snatches a dangerous weapon from the hands of her child. Let them know that all the secrets she hides are so many evils from which she protects them, and that the very difficulty they find in acquiring knowledge is not the least of her bounty towards them. Men are perverse; but they would have been far worse, if they had had the misfortune to be born learned.[4]

The old idea of Nature as left behind by Reason took on in Rousseau's thought overtones of nostalgia rather than celebration. The state of ignorance is presented as the lost paradise of natural man, haunting us as the image of a 'beautiful coast, adorned only by the hands of nature; towards which our eyes are constantly turned and which we see receding with regret'.[5] Humanity's distance from this idyllic past is measured in terms of the progress of Reason from Nature. In his speculative reconstruction of the history of the human race, in the *Discourse on the Origin of Inequality*, Rousseau presents the emergence of Reason as both the early flourishing of distinctively human nature and the beginning of its corruption. In the distant 'youth of the world', the capacity for self-improvement had drawn human beings out from the primitive state, where they seemed no different from other animals. This early form of distinctively human thought was an innocent thing, but it contained within it sources of inevitable corruption, and this prompted Rousseau to cry that reflection is the root of all ills and that the man who meditates is depraved. The interlude of innocent self-love, when human beings laid aside their original wildness – enjoying the advantages they had gained, singing and dancing around the oak trees – inevitably passed over into corrupting self-esteem.[6] They began to care who sang or danced the best; and in the cultivation of appearances, which was of the essence of *amour propre*, human beings lost contact with their true nature. From that point on, the progress of Reason, says Rousseau, reads like the history of an illness.

The moral of all this, Rousseau insisted at the end of the *Discourse on the Origin of Inequality*, is not that societies should be abolished and we return to the forests to live among bears.[7] Nostalgia was in fact only one side of his story of the development of Reason out of Nature and their subsequent interrelations. Reason was also the source of human renewal, of a genuine progress into a new and better 'natural' state. The emergence of self-consciousness, which began the 'history of illness', was at the same time a precondition for that ultimately happier state for humanity that is to be hoped for from the transformation of social institutions. Life in society is the source of human misery; but when properly reconstituted on rational principles, Rousseau says in *The Social Contract*, it is also the source of human ennoblement:

> The passage from the state of nature to the civil state produces a very remarkable change in man, by substituting justice for instinct in his conduct, and giving his actions a morality they had formerly lacked. Then only, when the voice of duty takes the place of physical impulses and right of appetite, does man, who so far had considered only himself, find that he is forced to act on different principles, and to consult his reason before listening to his inclinations. Although, in this state, he deprives himself of some advantages which he got from nature, he gains in return

others so great, his faculties are so stimulated and developed, his ideas so extended, his feelings so ennobled, and his whole soul so uplifted, that, did not the abuses of this new condition often degrade him below that which he left, he would be bound to bless continually the happy moment which took him from it forever, and instead of a stupid and unimaginative animal, made him an intelligent being and a man.[8]

In trying to specify the proper relations between Reason and Nature, Rousseau, unlike Bacon, was not concerned with the right epistemological framework for science. He points out in the preface to the *Discourse on the Origin of Inequality* that his enterprise – the understanding of natural man – cannot be readily accommodated to the methods of scientific enquiry. There is an unavoidable paradox in applying to the study of human nature the same methods which have so advanced knowledge in the natural sciences: man, the investigator, is very far removed from man, the object of enquiry. Man in his natural state can be studied only by man out of the state of nature; and the sophistication of his methods takes him still further from the state which ought to be the object of his study.

As every advance made by the human species removes it still further from its primitive state, the more discoveries we make, the more we deprive ourselves of the means of making the most important of all. Thus it is in one sense by our very study of man that knowledge of him is put out of our power.[9]

But Rousseau's reconstruction of man in his natural state is not really a scientific project; his concept of the natural operates as a means of social criticism rather than scientific investigation. The characteristics of natural man are determined by evaluating contemporary forms of social organization. 'There is, I feel, an age at which the individual man would wish to stop: you are about to inquire about the age at which you would have liked your whole species to stand still'.[10] The project is a critique of existing forms of social organization, with a view to better enabling human beings to live freely and naturally. The character ideals that issue from Rousseau's concept of Nature, unlike Bacon's, are not ideals for the good scientist, but for the good citizen; and they involve a reordering of the relations between Reason and Nature.

Rousseau retained Bacon's ideal of the attentive consideration of Nature; but his conception of the proper relationship between Reason and Nature in some ways reversed Bacon's. Through cultivation of Reason, human life becomes an expression of Nature; and Rousseau's version of this went beyond the ideal of Nature as exemplar to human conduct. He saw Nature not just as an external blueprint for human life, but as its inner truth. Nature is both the model and the source of an unspoiled simplicity and spontaneity which will break the bonds of distorting convention and artificiality. Living in contemporary society has removed human beings from their true nature. 'Politeness requires this thing; decorum that; ceremony has its forms and fashion its laws, and these we must always follow, never the promptings of our own nature.'[11] Reason must come to express the natural rather than the corrupted. And Rousseau saw its point of connection with the natural not as intellect, but as feeling. We live in accordance with Nature by letting Reason emerge from what we find in our own hearts.

Nature thus became for Rousseau a model for, and source of, moral regeneration. And the idea – and the ideals – of Reason changed accordingly. But despite this departure from the idea of progress through the subjugation of Nature, his versions of Reason and Nature retained a complex interdependence and interaction. Reason was supposed to model itself on Nature and to confine itself to expressing Nature's deliverances, received through the inner voice of the heart. It was supposed to be governed by Nature; but it continued, in a different way, to govern Nature itself. For Rousseau's Reason and Nature are not equal, independent terms, complete in themselves; and their interdependence is quite complex. He presents Nature as the most important partner in the coalition. Reason should be held in check by Nature; it expresses and transforms natural feeling, but remains under its rule. Closeness to Nature is the mark of what is true in Reason, as opposed to what is false and factitious. But in a different way – as the education of the young Emile shows – Rousseau's Reason also governs Nature, drawing out what is judged worthy of cultivation.

Rousseau depicts the right relation between Reason and Nature in his description of the natural garden in *The New Héloise*. According to the heroine Julie, those who love Nature, but cannot seek it in faraway places 'are reduced to doing it violence, to forcing it in some manner to come and dwell with them, and all this cannot be effected without a little illusion'.[12] In Julie's garden, 'nature has done everything', but under the firm direction of Julie herself; there is nothing the gardener has not ordered. Julie's cultivation, guided by the model of how Nature does things, but also guiding the unruly growth of Nature into an ordered pattern, epitomizes Rousseau's ideal. Nature needs to be tamed and ordered; but at the same time it provides the model for the gardener's cunning handiwork. Rousseau's Reason is modelled on Nature and is also its natural development. The rational is there within Nature, waiting to be drawn out; it is what the natural will be when properly developed.

Femininity is slotted into this complex dialectic of Rousseau's Reason–Nature relationship. Women symbolize a desired closeness to Nature which, in a sense, they never leave. They have the same ambiguous status as Nature in Julie's garden. Rousseau sees them as a potential source of disorder, as needing to be tamed by Reason. 'Never has a people perished from an excess of wine; all perish from the disorder of women', he complains in the *Letter to d'Alembert*.[13] But they are also, through their very closeness to Nature, objects of adulation and an inspiration to virtue. 'What man can be such a barbarian as to resist the voice of honour and reason, coming from the lips of an affectionate wife?' he asks in the dedication to the *Discourse on the Origin of Inequality*. 'Amiable and virtuous daughters of Geneva, it will be always the lot of your sex to govern ours.'[14]

We will see later the part played by this adulation of the feminine in Rousseau's treatment of morals and politics. For Rousseau, Nature is both a nostalgically remembered mythical past of the human species and a goal to be reattained, in a better form, through the ideal kind of Reason. This dual location of Nature creates new possibilities for woman as symbol. Female closeness to Nature enables woman to function as moral exemplar; she is both what Reason leaves behind and that to which it aspires. But it is men who make Rousseau's journey from corrupted Reason to Nature. It is they who enact the full drama of Reason's transformation so that it reflects and enhances true human nature. Rousseau's women never really make the journey; for them, unlike men, closeness to Nature is a natural state, not an achievement of Reason.

Kant: from immaturity to enlightenment

Later in the eighteenth century, Kant further developed the more optimistic, forward-looking strand in Rousseau's treatment of the place of Reason in human progress. He addressed himself to the place of Reason in the history of the human race in two short pieces published in 1784 – 'The idea for a universal history from a cosmopolitan point of view' and 'An answer to the question "What is Enlightenment?"' Here Kant sees the progress of Reason as assured by an encompassing and sustaining Nature, which is itself rational. Rousseau's theme of the subordination of human reason to Nature takes on in these pieces a teleological dimension. In 'The idea for a universal history', Kant presents Nature as a guiding force which gives human reason a purpose beyond any actual human intention.[15] 'Individual men and even entire nations little imagine that, while they are pursuing their own ends, each in his own way and often in opposition to others, they are unwittingly guided in their advance along a course intended by nature.'[16] What seems 'confused and fortuitous' in the actions of individuals can be seen in the history of the species as a 'steadily advancing but slow development of man's original capacities'. Human beings frequently act with no apparent rational purpose, but the philosopher should look for a 'purpose in nature' behind this 'senseless course of human events'.

Kant's optimism is grounded in an elucidation of the nature of human reason, and in a conviction of the rationality of Nature. Reason enables human beings to extend the rules and intentions they follow far beyond the limits of natural instinct; but it does not itself work instinctively. It requires trial, practice and instruction for its progress. Thus a long series of generations, each passing on its enlightenment to the next, is necessary to develop the 'germs implanted by nature in our species'. To suppose that these germs were not fully developed would be to suppose that Nature itself was not fully rational. If purposes were left unfulfilled, we would be faced not with a 'law-governed nature', but with an 'aimless, random process'. The 'dismal reign of chance' would replace the 'guiding principle of reason'. So, if we are to reconcile the nature of human reason with the rationality of Nature, we must see human history as a gradual progression towards the full realization of human capacities for Reason.

In this vision of human history Kant, like Rousseau, sees the capacity for self-improvement as the distinguishing feature of humanity. It is rational self-esteem, rather than mere well-being, that is the mark of human progress: 'nature does not seem to have been concerned with seeing that man should live agreeably, but with seeing that he should work his way onwards to make himself by his own conduct worthy of life and well-being.'[17] This means that the follies, malice and destructiveness of civilized behaviour, which made Rousseau look back with nostalgia to the 'lost youth of the world', should be seen as making possible the development of the species. Rousseau's insight into the ennobling potential of discord is developed by Kant into a celebration of social antagonism as the necessary precondition for the development of man's innate rational capacities. The 'unsocial sociability' of conflict and resistance awakens man's powers, enabling him to take the first steps from barbarism to social worthiness. Discord, far from being a pretext for pessimism, is the source of all the culture and art which adorn mankind, and of genuine morality. Without it, man would live an 'Arcadian, pastoral existence of perfect concord, self-sufficiency and natural love', but human talents would remain dormant: 'men as good-natured as the sheep they tended, would scarcely render their existence more valuable than that of their animals.' The end for which they were created – their rational nature – would be an 'unfilled void'.

> Nature should thus be thanked for fostering social incompatibility, enviously competitive vanity, and insatiable desires for possessions or even power. Without these desires, all man's excellent natural capacities would never be roused to develop. Man wishes concord, but nature, knowing better what is good for his species, wishes discord.[18]

Kant thus diagnosed Rousseau's apparent preference for the state of savagery as resting on an inadequately short-term view of the development of the species.

> We are *cultivated* to a high degree by art and science. We are *civilised* to the point of excess in all kinds of social courtesies and proprieties. But we are still a long way from the point where we would consider ourselves *morally* mature.[19]

The theme of moral maturity and its connections with the progress of Reason is further developed in 'What is Enlightenment?'[20] On Kant's definition, enlightenment consists in 'man's emergence from his self-incurred immaturity', from the inability, stemming from lack of resolution or courage, to use one's own understanding without the guidance of another. The motto of the Enlightenment is therefore: '*Sapere aude*! Have courage to use your *own* understanding.' Laziness and cowardice are the explanation of the fact that such a large proportion of humanity, 'including the entire fair sex', fall so readily under the sway of the 'guardians' who take it upon themselves to provide them with supervision. The general enlightenment of a society demands an end to such tutelage.

Kant's theme of enlightenment as maturity is associated with spatial metaphors as well as temporal ones. It involves access to a public space of autonomous speech; it depends on recognition of the 'freedom to make *public use* of one's reason in all matters'. Kant associates the coming-of-age of Reason with this distinctive public use of freedom, in which men of learning address a 'reading public'. The private use of Reason, exerted in civil posts or offices, can in contrast be narrowly restricted and controlled without detriment to the progress of enlightenment. Thus Kant thinks it is quite right that the State demand passive obedience from its functionaries, but these same functionaries, as 'men of learning', should be free to argue and criticize the workings of the State. The maturity proper to enlightenment is directly connected with access to a public space in which men of learning enjoy unlimited freedom to use their own reason and 'speak in their own person'. To restrict freedom in this sphere would be to 'virtually nullify a phase in man's upward progress, thus making it fruitless and even detrimental to subsequent generations'. It would be to 'violate and trample underfoot the sacred rights of mankind'.

Apart from his passing reference to the inclusion of 'the entire fair sex' in the guardians' exploitation of laziness and cowardice, Kant does not explore the possibility of a sexual differentiation in the process of enlightenment. However, by his own logic, the immaturity of women must be connected with their systematic exclusion both from the private use of Reason in the duties of civil functionaries, and from the public use of Reason, in which those roles are set aside. There is more at stake in this than the exclusion of women from the actual public places of learning and debate. The metaphor of a common intellectual space, which Kant evokes in this essay, is implicit also in his more formal treatments of morals. Ethical consciousness, like the 'enlightenment' Kant talks of here, involves an emergence from the subjectivity of immature consciousness into a public space of universal principles, autonomously pursued.

His ethical writings develop this theme into a view of morality as the antithesis of inclinations and feelings – a transcending of the subjectivity and particularity of passion to enter, as free consciousnesses, the common space of Reason.

Moral distinctions do not derive, as Hume had argued, from the operations of passion, diversifying human life. What is genuinely ethical about an act derives from its falling under rational, universalizable principles, which are binding regardless of the disparate desires and emotions which differentiate and divide rational beings. Kant's thought here echoes his claim in 'What is Enlightenment?' that Reason must find its full expression not in what pertains to the individual, but in the species. It is in what characterizes him as a rational being – what can be specified for all human beings indiscriminately – that a human being attains the status of a genuinely moral agent. The test of the morality of his acts is that they fall under abstract universal principles binding on rational agents as such.

In thus emphasizing universal principles, Kant restores to Reason the central place in morality which Hume had denied it. Like Hume, he thought that pure Reason had no power to know the real natures of things. In the *Critique of Pure Reason*, he argued that pure Reason is impotent in the theoretical sphere, for human knowledge depends on being given its objects from outside Reason. For human beings, the 'intuition' on which knowledge depends must be sensuous. Reason is a faculty of non-empirical, universal principles; but human knowledge depends on the senses. 'Reason', in Kant's sense, is thus confined, in the theoretical sphere, to mere thought; whereas 'understanding', operating in conjunction with the senses, yields genuine knowledge of the world as it must appear to rational beings constituted as we are. But the impotence which thus characterizes pure Reason in its theoretical use does not, for Kant, apply in the 'practical' sphere. Here Reason of itself yields moral principles, universally valid regardless of contingent empirical inclinations, passions or interests.

This limited picture of an austere moral agent in some respects does less than justice to Kant's intentions. His point was not that genuinely moral agents must shed their natural inclinations, desires and affections, but rather that what is distinctively moral about their actions can – contrary to Hume – be expressed entirely in terms of rational principles. None the less, his philosophy has fostered a view of morality which tends – as did Descartes's view of the self, which it in some ways resembles – to split human life, on the one hand, into truly moral universal concerns, and, on the other, into the particularities of the merely personal. On Kant's view, moral consciousness pertains to what is common to all human minds. But his version of morality – like Descartes's view of the mind – has nevertheless been caught up in the articulation of sexual difference. Ironically, the Kantian picture of morality, with its emphasis on what is supposedly universal about the mind, has been a major strand in more recent ideas of the lesser moral development of women. There are, for example, echoes of Kant's contrast between mere inclinations and the impersonality of duty in Freud's notorious claim that the moral development of women falls short of the full moral consciousness of men.

I cannot evade the notion (though I hesitate to give it expression) that for women the level of what is ethically normal is different from what it is in men. Their super-ego is never so inexorable, so impersonal, so independent of its emotional origins as we require it to be in men. Character traits which critics of every epoch have brought up against women – that they show less sense of justice than men, that they are less ready to submit to the great exigencies of life, that they are more often influenced in their judgments by feelings of affection or hostility – all these would be amply accounted for by the modification in the formation of their super-ego.[21]

Freud's assessment of the moral capabilities of women is expressed in terms of the superior male development of the super-ego through surmounting the oedipus complex. But, for all its novelty, his idea of male moral consciousness as an attainment is just a variant on an older pattern. The oedipus complex represents the point of access to the public space of Reason, the realm of universal principles in which genuine ethical consciousness operates; and male emergence from the oedipus complex is presented as a breaking away from the sway of the emotional and personal, from the subjectivity of mere 'feelings of affection or hostility'. The underlying picture of morality which is operating here is the highly influential one which found its fullest expression in Kant's ethics. Space was created within our intellectual tradition for the idea of the moral immaturity of female consciousness by the conception of Reason as developing from lesser forms of consciousness. This idea was pushed to its limits by Hegel.

Hegel: Reason as the unfolding of Nature

Rousseau's nostalgia for the receding coastline itself receded in Kant's confident affirmation of the progress of Reason under the benevolent guidance of Nature. But it was Hegel who brought to its fullest expression the theme of Reason's ultimate reconciliation with Nature. For him, the consciousness of individual minds, the progress of Reason and the development of human history are all part of a grand unfolding of Nature into its self-conscious realization as the Absolute. All apparent opposition between Mind and Nature is just a reflection of immature stages in the process of Nature's gradual unfolding and return to itself. As Hegel expresses the point in the *Phenomenology of Spirit*, what at first sight seems to happen outside Mind, and independent of it, is in fact its own doing. The agonizing sense of Reason's separation from Nature, which made Rousseau deplore the 'tyranny of reflection', was for Hegel just a mark of an immature form of Reason, which had not yet fully grasped its oneness with reality. The real is the rational and the rational the real; Reason and Nature are one. But it is only in the more advanced stages of consciousness that this is understood.

Hegel, like Rousseau and Kant before him, saw the progress of Reason in terms of the consciousness of freedom – a freedom whose mark was self-imposed obedience to law. In the *Social Contract*, Rousseau equated liberty with obedience to a law that we prescribe to ourselves.[22] And Kant developed this theme, identifying moral consciousness with the autonomy of Reason – the grasp of universalizable, formal principles, which transcend the particularity and partiality of feelings. Hegel, too, saw the progress of Reason as an advance into a freedom which rests on a greater comprehension of the universal – a detachment from the subjective and particular. But his development of the theme occurs in a framework which makes possible a much subtler accommodation between different stages in the advance of consciousness. In the *Phenomenology of Spirit*, he presents Nature as unfolding through Reason into Spirit in successive stages of human consciousness and their embodiment in social structures. Each stage is preserved and subsumed in the next. The less advanced forms of consciousness find their rationale in – and indeed are constituted by – those that come later. Reason moves on from its concealment within Nature through a vaguely apprehended sense of the unity of the real and the rational, to become Spirit, 'when its certainty of being all reality has been raised to truth, and it is conscious of itself as its own world, and of the world as itself'.[23] Rousseau's vague ideal of a kind of Reason that would draw out what is immanent in Nature, while remaining close to it, now attained a more explicit formulation.

Hegel tells the story of the progress of Reason both as the development of individual self-consciousness and as the development of forms of social organization. In both cases, relations of superseding hold between the less and more advanced stages. Each is what it truly is only in being superseded; the inner nature of each is discernible in the stage that lies beyond it. This theme is a recurring motif in Hegel's thought. And it produces rich and complex patterns of relationship between different forms of consciousness, enabling 'immature' stages to be both preserved and transcended. The pattern and its potential can be seen clearly in Hegel's account of the state of tormented awareness, which he calls the 'unhappy consciousness', and of the eventual resolution of its inner conflict.[24]

The unhappy consciousness incorporates both a sense of the unchangeableness of things, enshrined in 'stoicism', and a sense of the changeableness of things, enshrined in 'scepticism'. But it experiences their combination only in a consciousness of self as a 'dual-natured, merely contradictory being'. It grasps the resolution of its contradiction only in a vague sense that the unchangeable is in fact its own self. This is the state of devotion, a movement towards thought, whose 'thinking as such is no more than the chaotic jingling of bells, or a mist of warm incense, a musical thinking that does not get as far as the Notion'. It is a movement of infinite yearning of the pure heart, which feels itself as agonizingly self-divided. More advanced stages resolve this torment in more articulate awareness of the unity, underlying the surface contrast, between the changeability of Mind and the fixity of Nature. But they do not thereby disown as alien to them the less developed forms of consciousness that precede them.

Hegel's Spirit, echoing Kant's definition of enlightenment, 'calls to *every* consciousness: *be for yourselves* what you all are *in yourselves – reasonable*'.[25] But the importance of less enlightened forms of consciousness is now subtly preserved. There is no question that 'Reason should give up again the spiritually developed consciousness it has acquired, should submerge the widespread wealth of its moments again in the simplicity of the natural heart, and relapse into the wilderness of the nearly animal consciousness, which is also called Nature or innocence'.[26] But the very process of being superseded preserves and indeed constitutes them. They exist only as superseded. Thus Hegel makes it possible to present some forms of consciousness as immature in relation to others, but allows them to be preserved and acknowledged as well.

Gender does not figure explicitly in Hegel's story of the development of human consciousness in the early parts of the *Phenomenology of Spirit*. But the pattern he introduces there lends itself to the accommodation, containment and transcending of feminine consciousness, in relation to more mature 'male' consciousness. The stage is set for woman to be presented as being what she truly is only by virtue of what lies beyond her. In the next chapter we will see how, later in the work, Hegel explicitly relates femininity to comparatively immature stages in the advance of Reason.

5
The public and the private

Introduction: complementary consciousnesses

In Virginia Woolf's novel *Night and Day*, the heroine Katherine Hilbery indulges a secret passion for mathematics, retreating from the emotional complexities and responsibilities of female life into a furtive contemplation of abstract symbols and geometrical figures. For Katherine, this unfeminine activity represents clarity, impersonality and necessity, as against the engulfing confusion and contingency of domestic life. The familiar female longing which Virginia Woolf here describes goes beyond a desire for escape from the frequently crushing boredom and claustrophobia of a life spent entirely in the private domain. It is a longing also for release from a certain style of thought, from intellectual confinement to a realm of the particular, the merely contingent; a longing, in brief, for access to Reason. For Reason is the prerequisite for, and point of access to, not just the public domain of political life, but a realm of thought – of universal principles and necessary orderings of ideas. We saw that for Descartes right reasoning involved a struggle away from the sensuous and – at its limits – a complete detachment from the complexities and particularities of ordinary living. The goal of this arduous exercise remained in some ways continuous with the old Greek ideal of an ordered realm of thought, although the promised land was no longer the Platonic realm of universal forms, but rather the necessary principles of thought, supposedly the same for all minds.

The idea that women have their own distinctive kind of intellectual character or mode of thought is a relatively recent one in our philosophical tradition. Philo, Augustine and Aquinas, as we have seen, all presented femininity as somehow derivative in relation to a male paradigm of rational excellence. But they did not articulate this in terms of a complementarity between distinctively male and female intellectual character; women were seen as inferior in relation to a single standard of perfection. By the middle of the eighteenth century, we can detect a different note. Rousseau, for example, saw the minds of men and women as quite different in ways that make them 'complementary'. Each sex, pursuing the 'path marked out for it by nature', he says in Book V of *Emile*, is more perfect in that very divergence than if it more closely resembled the other. 'A perfect man and a perfect woman should no more be alike in mind than in face, and perfection admits of neither less nor more.'[1] He saw this complementarity relationship as implying the inappropriateness to women of the male style of intellectual functioning. 'The search for abstract and speculative truths, for principles and axioms in science, for all that tends to wide generalisation, is beyond a woman's grasp.'[2]

In his *Essay on the Sublime and the Beautiful*, Kant echoed Rousseau in insisting that although the fair sex has just as much understanding as the male, theirs is a different kind of understanding – a beautiful understanding. 'Laborious learning' or 'painful pondering', he suggested, destroys the merits that are proper to the female sex. A woman who attempts to be learned 'might as well even have a beard; for perhaps that would express more obviously the mien of profundity for which she strives'.[3] However, her lack of abstract thought is not regarded as a void in the female mind. What she lacks in the way of a grasp of universals, woman makes up in her possession of other mental traits – taste, sensibility, practical sense, feeling. Like Rousseau, Kant saw the complementary characters of male and female as together making up a single moral being: 'In matrimonial life the united pair should, as it were, constitute a single moral person, which is animated and governed by the understanding of the man and the taste of the wife.'[4]

Such complementation is supposed to be to the advantage of both sexes, although from Kant's description the gains do seem to be slanted towards the male. Through it, he becomes more perfect as a man; whereas the woman becomes more perfect as a wife. The male, again, is taken as the norm. In practice, this moral division of labour – as Mary Wollstonecraft pointed out in exasperation with Rousseau – may be a somewhat cumbersome arrangement. When both together make up but one moral being, the husband may be not always at hand to lend his wife his reason when it is most needed for such tasks as the right upbringing of children.

> Perchance his abstract reason, that should concentrate the scattered beams of her practical reason, may be employed in judging of the flavour of wine, descanting on the sauces most proper for turtle; or, more profoundly intent at a card-table, he may be generalizing his ideas as he bets away his fortune, leaving all the *minutiae* of education to his helpmate, or to chance.[5]

But however impractical the arrangement might be, this idea of a complementary character was supposed to be a compliment to the female sex. Women's lack of the cold and speculative forms of thought was for Rousseau and Kant associated with an adulation of them. This helped mask the fact that the supposedly distinctive intellectual character of women resulted from their exclusion from a male attainment. The situation is clearer in the more scornful version of female character offered later by Schopenhauer. In his essay *On Women*, he presents women's lack of reasoning powers as a kind of inherent immaturity. They can attain, he thinks, to reason only of a very limited sort and hence remain 'big children, their whole lives long'.[6]

In the *Philosophy of Right*, as we have seen, Hegel makes the same connection between what is distinctive about female consciousness and women's exclusion from a male attainment. And in the *Phenomenology of Spirit*, he shows an acute awareness of just how complex that exclusion is: 'womankind' is constituted through suppression.[7] Hegel's diagnosis of the constitution of womankind, through the divisions of public and private domains, reiterates, but also clarifies, an ambivalence towards the feminine which was already present in the thought of Rousseau. To get Hegel's insight into perspective, we must first see how Rousseau's views on Nature were related to his treatment of the public–private distinction.

For Rousseau, as we have seen, women's closeness to Nature made them moral exemplars, while at the same time it provided a rationale for their exclusion from citizenship. The containment of women in the domestic domain helped control the destructive effects of passion on civil society, while yet preserving it as an important dimension of human well-being. For it is not just the disorder of women associated with undisciplined passion that Rousseau saw as a threat to the public life of citizenship. Even the virtues associated with women's maternal feelings can threaten the proper functioning of the State, as emerges in the story of the Spartan mother in the opening sections of *Emile*. The good citizen gives thanks for the death of sons, if it serves the public good. Even virtuous passion can conflict with the demands of the State. The prerequisites for being a good private person are not fully consistent with those for being a good public citizen. Rousseau's solution, of course, was to make the men good citizens and the women good private persons. But he saw the two spheres as intersecting in ways that gave women a role in the development and preservation of good forms of public life, in which they themselves did not directly participate. The private was for Rousseau a domain of private virtue, free of the falseness and corruption of public life, under the reign of women close to Nature. And it was not merely a retreat for men from the corruption of contemporary society; it was also the nursery of good citizens who would transform public life.

The private domain thus formed an integral part of Rousseau's ideal for social relations. On the one hand, it served to keep women out of the public sphere. On the other, it served to contain passion and render it harmless to public order; it was both a haven of virtue and tenderness, from corrupt public life, and the model for its transformation. And in this realm of virtuous passion women were to preside. Rousseau's private women influence public political life through men. 'Nurtured in childhood' and 'tended in manhood' by virtuous women, men bring to the public domain a Reason governed by Nature. But the education of Sophie, described in Book V of *Emile*, makes it clear that this exemplary female virtue is largely a product of externally imposed restraint. Virtuous passion, on which Reason must model itself, is at the same time passion restrained. And the restraint incorporated into Sophie's education goes well beyond the tutor's intrusions on Emile's spontaneity in the course of his 'natural' education. Sophie's education is directed towards the flourishing of Emile's nature, in relation to which her own is complementary.

Rousseau repudiated the dichotomies between pure thought and bodily passion or sensuousness – associated especially with Descartes's theory of mind – in favour of a view of Reason as continuous with and guided by Nature. But his own complex ordering of Reason, passion and gender produced its own dichotomies – between male Reason and female passion – supposedly grounded in the difference between 'equal', but 'complementary' characters. The complementarity between male and female character is mapped onto the public–private distinction; and the interrelationship of the two domains ensures the flourishing of a truly natural and fully human

Reason. The content of Reason and its relations with Nature changed, but the organization of male and female roles around these concepts remained fundamentally the same.

We saw in Chapter 3 that women occur, perforce, also on the private side of Hume's very different version of the public–private distinction, although not in the explicit way in which Rousseau assigns them their place. Where Hume does explicitly discuss male–female relations, the associations of femininity are very different from Rousseau's idyllic domestic retreats. In his *Essays*, women are associated with a wider domain of reflective social intercourse – an urbane, civilized social life, of a kind for which Rousseau professed only scorn. In his essay on 'Essay writing' Hume, in light-hearted gallantry, associates women, to their advantage, with the urbane 'conversible' as distinct from the sterile 'learned' world.[8] The proper exercise of reflective thought demands not withdrawal from, but rather a close involvement with, 'common life and conversation'. It is a merit of his times, he suggests, that they have seen emerge a 'league between the learned and conversible worlds'. Intellectual life is at its best when not divorced from conversation and common life. And the conversible world, he ironically suggests, is the special domain of women.

The conversible world is neither the private haven of domesticated passion nor the nether world we will see in Hegel's account of Family Life, removed from the light of society. The female objects of Hume's ironic gallantry are, none the less, in something of a twilight zone. They have no place either in the private activities of civil society, where male household heads pursue the acquisition of goods and possessions; or in the creation and preservation of the moral dimension of public society, where private acquisitiveness is restrained by wider forms of self-interest. Both forms of the public–private distinction are assimilated into Hegel's startling formulations of the relations between the feminine nether world and the light of day, and of the constitution of womankind through suppression.

Hegel: the feminine nether world

In his discussion of the Family in the *Phenomenology of Spirit*, Hegel draws together several themes we have already looked at: the idea of Family Life as a retreat to particularity, the distinction between a private and a public pursuit of power and wealth, the distinction between less and more advanced stages of consciousness, the distinction between 'natural' feeling and 'universal' ethical consciousness. He also adds something new, although it can be seen as germinally present in Kant's public space of autonomous speech: the distinction between the 'outer', as the realm of actuality, and the shadowy and insubstantial 'inner', which finds its reality only through externalization. And he explicitly aligns the feminine with the private side of this enriched public–private distinction.

Hegel equates female consciousness with the life of the Family, a primitive stage in relation to the more self-conscious life of Civil Society.[9] They both form part of 'ethical life', which is an early stage in the unfolding of Spirit in social, cultural and political life; in response to inner tensions, ethical life passes over into more advanced stages of Spirit's self-realization, such as law. These inner tensions take the form of conflict between human law, identified with Civil Society and men, and divine law, identified with the Family and women. The Family represents the unconscious notion of the ethical, as opposed to its self-conscious existence embodied in the wider life of Society, where the ethical 'shapes and maintains itself by working for the universal'.

The ethical principle, both in the Family and in wider Society, is intrinsically universal, transcending the particularity of mere feeling. Thus, in so far as the Family is construed as embodying ethical life, it already involves universality. But the ethical character of Family Life is superseded by – and hence, for Hegel, dependent on – the Family's involvement through the husband in a life external to the Family. In the wider public arena, the male pursues on behalf of the Family the acquisition and maintenance of power and wealth; and this public activity transcends its significance for the private gain of the individual and his family. The enterprise takes on a higher determination which does not fall within the Family itself, but bears on what is truly universal – the community. In relation to the Family, this external activity of the male has in fact a negative role, 'expelling the individual from the Family, subduing the natural aspect and separateness of his existence, and training him to be virtuous, to a life in and for the universal'.[10]

Divine law, embodied in the Family, is concerned with duties and affections towards blood relatives. All this Hegel sums up as the 'nether world'; and because women are not citizens, it is also the domain of women. For them there is no actual participation in the forms of Spirit which go beyond Family Life. This is not, for Hegel, a matter of excluding women from the ethical order. Ethical life does occur within the Family; and despite their confinement to it, women can be concerned with the universal, rather than with the particularity of natural feeling. But because they lack access to that wider domain of self-conscious 'working for the universal', their ethical life involves a predicament which does not arise for men.

In the ethical household, it is not a question of *this* particular husband, *this* particular child, but simply of husband and children generally; the relationships of the woman are based, not on feeling, but on the universal. The difference between the ethical life of the woman and that of the man consists just in this, that in her vocation as an individual and in her pleasure, her interest is centred on the universal and remains alien to the particularity of desire; whereas in the husband these two sides are separated; and since he possesses as a citizen the self-conscious power of universality, he thereby acquires the right of desire and, at the same time, preserves his freedom in regard to it. Since, then, in this relationship of the wife there is an admixture of particularity, her ethical life is not pure; but in so far as it *is* ethical, the particularity is a matter of indifference, and the wife is without the moment of knowing herself as *this* particular self in the other partner.[11]

Hegel's point is that in so far as relations within the Family are particular – focused on this particular husband or child – they are not also ethical. Husbands, in contrast to wives, have an additional sphere of activity, where they 'work for the universal'. A man can thus treat his family relationships as entirely particular without sacrificing his ethical life. But a woman can have the ethical life only to the extent that she can transform the particularity of family relationships into ethical, universal concerns – for Husband and Children as such, rather than for these particular people. So what is particular for the male is universal and ethical for the female. And this gives rise, Hegel goes on to point out, to inevitable conflicts between men and women. From the perspective of the man, these are conflicts between the ethical and the merely particular. Family life drags him back to the particular from the outer realm of universality. But for the woman the conflicts take the form of external encroachments on the ethical demands of the Family.

Thus there is conflict between different embodiments of the ethical stage of Spirit, as 'male' and 'female' consciousness. Not just family concerns, but womankind itself, becomes the enemy of the wider community. It must be suppressed; and this suppression, as well as making possible the very existence of the community, also constitutes womankind as what it is. The stage of consciousness associated with the Family and women, like other immature stages of consciousness, exists precisely through being transcended.

Since the community only gets an existence through its interference with the happiness of the Family, and by dissolving (individual) self-consciousness into the universal, it creates for itself in what it suppresses and what is at the same time essential to it an internal enemy – womankind in general. Womankind – the everlasting irony (in the life) of the community – changes by intrigue the universal end of the government into a private end, transforms its universal activity into a work of some particular individual, and perverts the universal property of the state into a possession and ornament for the Family.[12]

Male and female consciousness share the complex interdependence of Civil Society and the Family, human and divine law. In being superseded, Hegel insists, the Family is not destroyed; it remains as the 'base', 'power' and 'authentication' of the next stage, on which, however, it depends for its own actuality.

Neither of the two is by itself absolutely valid; human law proceeds in its living process from the divine, the law valid on earth from that of the nether world, the conscious from the unconscious, mediation from immediacy – and equally returns whence it came. The power of the nether world, on the other hand, has its actual existence on earth; through consciousness, it becomes existence and activity.[13]

Likewise, the union of man and woman constitutes the 'active middle term' of the whole. It is through her relation to man that woman is part of the 'upward movement of the law of the nether world to the actuality of the light of day and to conscious existence'. And it is through his relation to the Family and the feminine that man is involved in the corresponding 'downward movement' from actuality to unreality.[14]

Within family life, ethical consciousness is always precarious – liable to lapse back into merely 'natural' feeling. It is through the brother–sister relationship, Hegel thinks, that women have most prospect of maintaining the required form of universal consciousness. Compared with her relations with husband, parents or children, a woman's relationship to a brother can be free from passion or distracting struggles for, or against, independence. But even in the relatively free brother–sister relationship, female ethical consciousness remains vague and shadowy when compared with what the brother can achieve by breaking away from the 'immediate, elemental, and therefore, strictly speaking, negative ethical life of the Family, in order to acquire and produce the ethical life that is conscious of itself and actual'.[15] In contrast to this masculine self-consciousness, the 'feminine in the form of the sister' is confined to 'the highest *intuitive* awareness of what is ethical'.

> She does not attain to *consciousness* of it, or to the objective existence of it, because the law of the Family is an implicit, inner essence which is not exposed to the daylight of consciousness, but remains an inner feeling and the divine element that is exempt from an existence in the real world.[16]

Hegel's theme of the dependence of the 'inner' and the 'outer' has been a preoccupation of more recent treatments of the relationship between public language and the inner life of the mind. Within his own system, it operates to make female consciousness derivative on the 'objective' existence of male consciousness in the real world. In Hegel's elegant containment of the feminine by more advanced forms of consciousness, woman's status as a rational, fully ethical being depends on her relationship to man. Here, as with Rousseau, woman is not a direct participant in the drama on which her nature depends. It is only by virtue of what transcends her that she is what she truly is.

Hegel's treatment of femininity, like Rousseau's, is double-edged. On the one hand, it functions as a rationalization of women's exclusion from the political domain. Women differ from men as 'plants differ from animals', as he expresses the point in the *Philosophy of Right*. The principle that underlies their development is the 'vague unity of feeling', rather than a grasp of universality. So when they hold the helm of government, the State is at once in jeopardy.[17] On the other hand, the associations of this immature stage of consciousness are not entirely negative. Hegel did not intend his descriptions of female consciousness to be dismissive of women. He saw the nether world as necessary to the wider life of Society. From the male perspective, its existence allows men to flourish as fully self-conscious ethical beings without sacrificing natural feeling. And from this perspective women can indeed be seen as in some respects morally superior to men; virtuous women make of the unpromising material of natural feeling and particular relationships something genuinely ethical and universal.

Womankind may be the irony of the State; but Hegel saw the family concerns it represented as also essential to the State. They are not to be rejected, but preserved in a higher synthesis. The prerogative of thus having it both ways is, however, a male one. 'Womankind' is constituted by male containment of the concerns of family into what is, for men, a domain of particularity, to which they can repair from their external activities. As Hegel's own analysis of the structural relationships between Family and Civil Society, Woman and Man, makes clear, it is nothing of the kind for women.

6
The struggle for transcendence

Introduction

In *The Second Sex*, Simone de Beauvoir complained that women 'have erected no virile myth in which their projects are reflected', that they 'still dream through the dreams of men'. And she linked this lack with a crucial failure in self-consciousness – with women's failure to set themselves up as Subject; their connivance at remaining 'other' in relation to men: 'A myth always implies a subject who projects his hopes and his fears towards a sky of transcendence.'[1] We have now seen some of the ways in which the western intellectual tradition's ideals of Reason have contributed to this female predicament. Women's general disinclination to reach for the sky of transcendence is connected not only with practical obstacles, but also with conceptual ones. The 'status of manhood' has been seen as itself an attainment, in ways in which femininity is not. Women have shared in these ideals only at the expense of their femininity, as culturally defined. And these definitions have intersected with articulations of the public–private distinction in ways that have helped form our understanding of femininity as a complement to male Reason – a domain of 'natural' concerns and traits, out of which men are expected to grow to maturity.

De Beauvoir's ideal for women was that they should themselves break away from the 'immanence' in which they have been thus contained, to achieve their own transcendence – the state of self-definition and self-justification – through freely chosen 'projects and exploits'. Women should become free consciousnesses standing above the immanence of life. The ideal is expressed in terms of Sartre's existentialism of *Being and Nothingness*. But it derives also from Hegel's treatment of self-consciousness in the *Phenomenology of Spirit*, mediated through Sartre. For Hegel, selfhood is attained through transcending the immersion of unreflective consciousness in mere living; it is a process which involves struggle – it arises from the inherently conflict-ridden relations of mutual recognition between different consciousnesses. This theme forms a major strand in de Beauvoir's conception of 'otherness', which she presents in *The Second Sex* as a basic trait of woman: the peculiar way in which a supposedly free and autonomous being finds herself compelled to assume the status of the Other in relation to another ego which is 'essential and sovereign'.[2] Woman as 'other' in this sense is stabilized as an object, doomed to 'immanence'; her transcendence is overshadowed and itself transcended by another consciousness.

In this chapter I want to trace de Beauvoir's diagnosis of the condition of women back to its Hegelian origins. In the process, we will see more clearly some of the tensions in de Beauvoir's ideal of a *feminine* transcendence; and also just how pervasive is the influence of past philosophical thought on contemporary character ideals, even where these are explicitly meant to repudiate sex bias.

Hegel: self-consciousness as achievement

Hegel dramatized the emergence of self-consciousness in his famous story of the master–slave struggle in the early sections of the *Phenomenology of Spirit*.[3] The story in some ways parallels the account we have already looked at, later in the work, of the emergence of self-conscious ethical life out of its unconscious form. Sustained self-consciousness emerges out of less advanced stages in the unfolding of Spirit. Two points about Hegel's treatment of this theme are important for our purposes: his understanding of the relationship between self-consciousness and life, and his claim that sustained self-consciousness presupposes a struggle between consciousnesses.

What is distinctive about self-certainty, as Hegel calls this stage of consciousness, is that it defines itself against life as its opposite. More primitive stages of consciousness consisted in awareness of determinate, but static objects, following external laws. The stage of self-certainty, in contrast, is associated with awareness of organic living things. It apprehends itself as set over against life, conceived as an 'infinite unity of differences'. It understands life as not exhausted by any of the particular determinate forms it takes on. This links self-consciousness with awareness of the possibility of death; and it also means that self-consciousness takes the form, not of bare awareness of things, but of desire. This transition sets the scene for Hegel's claim that self-consciousness involves an inevitable struggle between consciousnesses.

Self-consciousness, Hegel insists, demands inter-subjective awareness. An isolated consciousness cannot sustain self-consciousness. It can be aware of itself only by having consciousness presented to it as an outer object. But because this stage of developing consciousness takes the form of desire, a contradiction arises. The emerging self realizes that the object of its desire is independent of itself. The object is an 'other' and its otherness must be overcome if the truth of self-certainty – the sustained grasp of self as there in the world – is to be achieved. Even the lower forms of life, Hegel quaintly observes, act in conformity with this need to supersede the other by making it a part of themselves; they devour what they need from the world. But for fully self-conscious beings the necessary incorporation of the other is a more complex task than eating. Self-consciousness is certain of itself only by overcoming the other, cancelling its otherness. The satisfaction of desire overcomes independent otherness. In destroying the independence of the other, a self objectifies its own self-consciousness as in the world. But this can now be seen as a self-defeating enterprise; for the very being of self-consciousness demands that there be an independent other to thus overcome. With the incorporation of the other, self-consciousness now disintegrates for want of an external consciousness in which its own being will be mirrored back to it.

Hegel's conclusion is that, if self-consciousness is to be sustained, the object set over against it must effect the required negation within itself. That is, it must allow itself to be incorporated without thereby ceasing to exist. The only way this can be achieved is through the recognition of one consciousness by another: 'Self-consciousness achieves its satisfaction only in another self-consciousness.' Consciousness here 'first finds its turning point, where it leaves behind it the colourful show of the sensuous here-and-now and the nightlike void of the supersensible beyond, and steps out into the spiritual daylight of the present.'[4]

It is the necessity of recognition that makes sustained self-consciousness inherently conflict-ridden. If self-consciousness is to be sustained, it must be, as it were, confronted by itself in another; there can be no self-consciousness without consciousness of the other. But this mutual need of the other's recognition – demanding, as it does, that each engage in its own negation in order to sustain the other's self-certainty – means that the two consciousnesses must 'prove themselves and each other through a life-and-death struggle'. The struggle may end in the actual death of one of the antagonists. However, the more interesting outcome, which makes possible a transition to richer forms of consciousness, is that wherein both survive, but with one in a state of subjection to the other. Both have staked their lives, and by living through the fear of death they have attained to a kind of consciousness which transcends mere absorption in the immediacy of life. They are now conscious of life as something not exhausted by any of the particular determinate forms it takes. Hegelian self-certainty is grounded in this detached awareness; it stands above life, rather than being absorbed in it, as are the lesser forms of consciousness. But the two consciousnesses in Hegel's story are transformed in different ways by the fear of death they have each lived through. They survive as different kinds of self-consciousness: master and slave.

It now turns out that, from the point of view of the master, the existence of the subjected consciousness no longer serves the purpose for which it was needed. Self-consciousness was to be sustained through the satisfied desire for recognition; but the outcome of the struggle is a recognition that is 'one-sided and unequal'. The object in which the master has achieved his mastery is not an independent consciousness, but a servile one in which he cannot recognize himself; the required reflection of independent consciousness is distorted by the subjection which has been the condition of its attainment. So, despite his 'victory', the master has found no external object in which his free, independent consciousness can be mirrored and hence sustained. The kind of recognition he receives from the slave is in fact detrimental to the project of sustaining awareness of self as free independent consciousness; the self-certainty of the victor is once again under threat. Nor is this all there is to the souring of the master's victory. His relation to non-conscious things is now mediated through the slave's labour on them. He is thus deprived of what, for the slave, will prove the ultimately successful externalization of self – the capacity to labour on things and thus make them over in one's own form.

A corresponding reversal is the lot of the dependent consciousness of the slave. Whereas the externalized truth of the master's self-consciousness is the servile consciousness of the slave, that of the slave is the free consciousness of the master – at any rate, for as long as that free consciousness can be sustained.

The slave, moreover, is able, through his enforced labour on things, to transform his immediate relationship to the world into self-conscious awareness of it. Mere labouring on things, without having been through the life and death struggle, would leave consciousness immersed in the immediacy of lower forms of consciousness. But the slave has been through the fear of death, which has shaken everything stable in his world to its foundations. He is now aware of life as something not exhausted by the immediate and particular vanishing moments of experience. Labour itself now becomes a way of actually controlling the dissolution of stability, and reworking natural existence in the worker's own form. It becomes 'desire held in check, fleetingness staved off'. Through forming and shaping things, the slave's consciousness acquires what eludes the master – an element of permanence; he discovers himself in the forms his work imposes on objects.[5] Sustained self-consciousness demands an externalization of the self, so that it becomes possible to find self, as it were, in the outer world. Without such objectification, self-consciousness remains tenuous, liable to slip back into immersion in life.

The contrast between the externalization of self, which makes possible sustained self-consciousness, and immersion in life, which cannot sustain a stable self-consciousness, is echoed in Hegel's discussion of human and divine law. It is access to the wider life of Society, beyond the confines of the family, that sustains self-conscious ethical life. It demands an externalization into an outer realm beyond the particularities of family life. In the lack of that externalization, ethical consciousness remains tenuous and unstable, liable to lapse back into merely natural feelings. In so far as he is not a citizen, but belongs to the family, as we saw, the individual is only an 'unreal, impotent shadow'.

In the light of Hegel's treatment of male–female relations, how are we to understand the implications for gender of the earlier master–slave story? I suggest that the two struggles – master–slave and male–female – should be taken in conjunction. Each story illuminates the other, and what connects them is the theme of the conditions of sustained self-consciousness. Self-consciousness is associated with a breaking away (achieved through surviving the fear of death) from immersion in life and its particular transient attachments. And self-conscious ethical life is likewise associated with a breaking away from the family, which – at any rate from the male perspective – is also associated with particularity.

The point here is not that what awaits men beyond the confines of family life is a life and death struggle for recognition, issuing in master–slave relationships. The two stories do not intersect in that way. The male, when he leaves the constraints of family life, engages in civilized activities associated with the acquisition and maintenance of power and wealth. None the less, the stories map one another. The master–slave story describes a struggle for dominance between consciousnesses intent on obtaining recognition of a kind which will sustain self-certainty. The proper locus of sustained selfhood is not relationships of love associated with natural affections and particularity, but a struggle for mastery which is bound up with the capacity for detachment from mere living. And women are outside this drama; they belong in a different, 'inner' domain, which is not primarily associated with sustained self-consciousness.

The master–slave struggle is of course not formulated explicitly to exclude mistresses or female slaves. But, in the light of Hegel's later discussion of women, its overtones of maleness do not seem incidental. The struggle for sustained self-consciousness is really one between male selves and others. Women do not – at any rate in their own right – fit into this dialectic as either masters or slaves. They are, however, given a share in the spoils of victory. As we have already seen, through their relations to men, they are part of the 'upward movement' towards self-conscious existence.

We should, then, expect some oddities in any attempt to apply the relations of recognition between Hegelian selves and others to understanding the condition of women. And, as we shall see, some of the puzzling features of de Beauvoir's analysis of the female predicament do seem to derive from the underlying maleness of the original Hegelian confrontation of consciousnesses. However, de Beauvoir's application of Hegel's philosophy is taken not from the original version, but from Sartre's adaptation of it in *Being and Nothingness*, which differs from Hegel in some important and relevant respects.[6]

Sartre and de Beauvoir: women and transcendence

Sartre's version of the master–slave story highlights the theme of reciprocal recognition. The final stage of Hegel's story – the externalization of self through labour – drops out altogether. Moreover, Sartre gives his own twist to Hegel's description of the struggle for recognition. The power struggle becomes a struggle between competing 'looks'. Sartre is thus able to bring into the Hegelian confrontation between consciousnesses his own existentialist preoccupations with freedom and the transcendence of determinate situations. Only one of the antagonists in the life and death struggle, in Sartre's version of it, can be a looker; the other must be the looked-at. If the looker is a 'subject', the looked-at turns into an 'object'. So my awareness of being looked at can never give me a sense of myself as a subject. What I am aware of through that experience is not myself as a subjective being, but rather an objectified self – the 'self-for-others'. There is for Sartre no possibility of reciprocal recognition between transcendent selves. The look transforms its object in a 'radical metamorphosis' from a transcendent being into a degraded consciousness. Sartre brings out the crucial point here in a highly evocative section describing the contrasts between the experience of looking at someone who is not looking at me, and that of being myself looked at.[7]

I am to suppose myself in a public park. Not far away I see a lawn, and benches on its edge. I experience them as grouped towards me. But then a man passes by those benches, and the objects acquire an orientation which 'flees' from me. I experience a 'reorganization of space'. I am aware of a spatiality that is not mine: 'an object has appeared which has stolen the world from me.' The centralization of the world which I effect as perceiver is undermined: 'it appears that the world has a kind of drain hole in the middle of its being and that it is perpetually flowing off through this hole.' But all of this, so far, is contained within my centralization of the scene. This man who is effecting the 'internal haemorrhage' of my world is himself an object in my spatialization. The bleeding away of my world is controlled, localized. His look directed at other objects is itself contained in my world. The situation becomes quite different if he now looks at me; his look can no longer be contained as an object in a world centred around my own look.

The point Sartre extracts from all this is that we cannot perceive as an object a look fastened on us; it must be either one or the other. To apprehend a look directed at us is precisely not to apprehend an object; it is, rather, consciousness of being looked at. And it is this experience which yields the Sartrean other. 'The Other is in principle the One that looks at me.' The look that yields the sense of the other need not be 'the convergence of two ocular globes in my direction'. It can be a rustling of branches, the sound of a footstep followed by silence, the opening of a shutter, the movement of a curtain. This sense of the other's look is at the heart of such emotions as shame. Listening behind a door out of jealousy, I hear footsteps behind me and experience shame, which involves awareness of myself as object to the other. The immediate effect of this awareness is a denial of my transcendence, so that I become tied to a determinate nature. The look of the other fixes my possibilities. By denying my transcendence, it denies my freedom. I am placed in danger – a danger which is no accident, but the permanent structure of my being-for-others.[8] This is the state of slave consciousness in Sartre's version of the master–slave struggle. Whereas the consciousness of the master retains transcendence of all determinate situations, that of the slave is immersed in determinacy.

In Hegel's version of the story, both consciousnesses live through the fear of death; and it is the freedom this brings that later enables the slave to externalize self in the world through labour. In Sartre's version, the benefits of having staked one's life, and lived through the fear of death, accrue entirely to the master. They reside in the kind of self he is now perceived as being. My very existence as a self-conscious being, for Sartre, depends not just on the fact of the other's recognition, but on what kind of self the other recognizes me as being: 'As I appear to the Other, so I am.' So, to the extent that the other apprehends me as 'bound to a body and immersed in *life*', I am myself 'only *an Other*'. In order to make myself recognized by the Other, I must risk my own life: 'To risk one's life, in fact, is to reveal oneself as not-bound to the objective form or to any determined existence – as not-bound to life.' Sartrean slave consciousness remains immersed in life, as something too dear to lose; whereas the master, through risking life, being prepared to die, breaks free to stand above life, unconfined by the determinacies of his situation. He transcends all determination to any particular mode of existence. Sartre's version of the story thus expresses his own existentialist preoccupations with the theme of absolute freedom as the achievement of a transcendence of all determinate situations; and this becomes crucial in de Beauvoir's application of this framework to the condition of women. 'I have risked my life', the Sartrean master exults. On the other hand, 'the Other remains bound to external things in general; he appears to me and he appears to himself as *non-essential*. He is the *Slave*, I am the *Master*; for him, it is I who am essence.'[9]

Sartrean slave consciousness thus involves a fall from freedom into objectification. The look of the master transforms its object into a degraded consciousness. There is, however, for Sartre, something intrinsically false about this objectification. I cannot ultimately be deprived of my transcendence; for this would involve an alienation of selfhood. The other does not constitute me as an object for myself, but only for him. I take on, as it were, his alienating gaze; but I cannot really be alienated from myself. The objectifying force of the other's look can, in principle, always be resisted. My absolute freedom as a subject cannot ultimately be denied.

The resistance of the other's objectifying look is central to Sartre's version of the life and death struggle between rival consciousnesses. Each strives to be the one that retains freedom, turning the other into an object. It is impossible for both lookers to be reciprocally free, recognizing one another's 'being-for-self'. Thus the Sartrean antagonists struggle for the role of looker. Each consciousness rejects the other's objectifying look, refusing to be limited to what it is perceived as being. Sartrean selfhood essentially involves this constant wrenching away from the other's attempt to fix my possibilities by perceiving me as object; it involves a constant surpassing of fixed or 'dead' possibilities. The true Sartrean self is in this way a 'perpetual centre of infinite possibilities', which refuses to be known as an object. And it is this ideal of transcendence which de Beauvoir takes over in *The Second Sex*.

De Beauvoir on woman as other

De Beauvoir's idea of woman as other is articulated in terms drawn from the Sartrean struggle for dominance between looker and looked-at. There can at any one time be only one Sartrean looker; the other must be looked-at. In appropriating this point to the analysis of the female condition, de Beauvoir introduced two variations to the Sartrean theme. The first is that, with respect to relations between the sexes, one sex is, as it were, permanently in the privileged role of looker; the other is always the looked-at. The second is that in her version of the struggle between hostile consciousnesses one side connives in its defeat. Women are engaged in the struggle, but they are somehow not serious antagonists. Unlike the original master–slave struggle from which it all derives, the outcome here is not really a 'subjugation'. Women have themselves submitted to constitute a permanent Other.

In the Sartrean struggle, two consciousnesses are locked in a combat of fierce, uncompromising looks. The outcome is uncertain, although one must go under. In de Beauvoir's application of this model to the sexual division, woman connives at being the objectified Other. Women accept their own objectification, being well-pleased with the arrangement.

> To decline to be the Other, to refuse to be a party to the deal – this would be for women to renounce all the advantages conferred upon them by their alliance with the superior caste. Man-the-sovereign will provide woman-the-liege with material protection and will undertake the moral justification of her existence.[10]

De Beauvoir elaborates what makes this extraordinary arrangement appealing to women in terms drawn from Sartre's treatment of the demands of freedom. The condition of being female is interpreted as a permanent state of Sartrean 'bad faith', in which women connive at being turned into objects, denying their transcendence. The condition and its ideal alternative are expressed in terms of immanence and transcendence.

> Every subject plays his part as such specifically through exploits or projects that serve as a mode of transcendence; he achieves liberty only through a continual reaching out towards other liberties. There is no justification for present existence other than its expansion into an indefinitely open future. Every time transcendence falls back into immanence, stagnation, there is a degradation of existence into the '*en-soi*' – the brutish life of subjection to given conditions – and of liberty into constraint and contingence. This downfall represents a moral fault if the subject consents to it; if it is inflicted upon him, it spells frustration and oppression. In both cases it is an absolute evil. Every individual concerned to justify his existence feels that his existence involves an undefined need to transcend himself, to engage in freely chosen projects.[11]

Many contemporary readers of *The Second Sex* will have reservations about Sartrean transcendence as a human ideal, even apart from the limitations it may have as a feminist one. Can any will really be as free as Sartre would have it? And should we really want to be transcendent selves, leaping about in triumphant assertions of will in defiance of all the apparent determinacies in our situations? The ideal of radical freedom and the associated idea of bad faith can be seen, too, as in some ways just adding an extra burden of self-recrimination on those – male or female – who find themselves caught in oppressive situations. However, the queries I want to raise here concern more specifically what becomes of the Hegelian and Sartrean treatments of self-consciousness in de Beauvoir's analysis of the predicament of women.

First, let me stress what I regard as a positive feature of de Beauvoir's use of the original Hegelian framework, as mediated by Sartre. De Beauvoir is of course not explicitly addressing herself to Hegel's treatment of the condition of women. But her own account of the female predicament can, none the less, be seen as illuminating an inner tension in Hegel's position. Hegel did not regard women as lacking the status of spiritual subjects. It is true that he saw them as, in a sense, closer to Nature than men: the form of ethical life with which they are associated is a less advanced form of spirit than that associated with men. It is, none the less, supposed to be genuinely ethical. Woman does share in the more advanced stages of spirit; but, as we have seen, she does so in a curiously vicarious way, through her relations to man.

For de Beauvoir, as for Sartre, the conditions of selfhood are, in contrast, quite uncompromising. Nothing short of actual engagement in 'projects' and 'exploits' will do. In the lack of that, human subjects are forced back into mere immanence. There can be no vicarious selfhood; and it can be only through bad faith that women regard their relations to men as giving them a share in transcendence. The middle zone which Hegel sets aside for women – located between the merely 'natural' and full participation in the outer world of projects and exploits – must be seen as a delusion. If women are not out there engaging in their own projects and exploits, they are reduced to mere immanence or immersion in life. There is no middle zone between transcendence and immanence.

In this way, we can see de Beauvoir's treatment of the Otherness of women as drawing out the inner inconsistencies in Hegel's treatment of woman's status as a spiritual subject. However, this repudiation of the Hegelian nether world, as nothing but the zone of bad faith, has some more negative consequences for de Beauvoir's account of the condition of being female. They come out especially in some of her remarks about female biology, where she presents the female predicament as a conflict between being an inalienable free subject, reaching out to transcendence, and being a body which drags this subject back to a merely natural existence. It is as if the female body is an intrinsic obstacle to transcendence, making woman a 'prey of the species'. During menstruation, she says, a woman feels her body most painfully as an obscure, alien thing; it is indeed, the 'prey of a stubborn and foreign life....Woman, like man, *is* her body; but her body is something other than herself.'[12]

This apparently stark dualism between transcendence through the will and confinement to bodily immanence is a disconcerting picture of the condition of being female. At this point the notion of woman as other may well seem to have overreached itself. How can objectification of consciousness make one's very body other to oneself? Why should a woman's direct experience of her own body be an experience of lack of transcendence, of immersion in life? Why, at any rate, should this be so in any way that would not apply equally to the direct experience of a male body? Here it may well seem that de Beauvoir has appropriated, along with the Sartrean idea of transcendence, his notorious treatment of the female body as the epitome of immanence.[13]

In partial defence of de Beauvoir here, it can of course be said that the experience – however direct – of a female body which she is describing is the experience of a body which has been culturally objectified by exposure to the male look. De Beauvoir warns her readers that her use of the words *woman* or *feminine* are not intended to refer to any changeless essence; that the reader must understand the phrase 'in the present state of education and custom' after most of her statements.[14] And there is certainly something correct about the suggestion that women experience even their own bodies in ways that reflect the conditioning effects of a male objectifying look.

It is not female biology itself, we may say, that poses the obstacle to a feminine transcendence, but rather what men, with the connivance of women, have made of female biology. And de Beauvoir does seem to have this distinction clearly in mind in the following passage:

> Men have presumed to create a feminine domain – the kingdom of life, of immanence – only in order to lock up women therein....What they demand today is to be recognized as existents by the same right as men and not to subordinate existence to life, the human being to its animality.[15]

But perhaps there is more to it than this. What makes the female body such a threat to Sartrean transcendence seems to be not just the result of its having been objectified by the male look. Underlying de Beauvoir's descriptions of female biology is the original Hegelian opposition between the individuality of self-consciousness and the inchoate generality of life. It is not just for straightforward practical reasons that woman's greater biological involvement in 'species life' poses obstacles to her attaining transcendence. It is not just that, given the prevailing modes of social organization, woman's primary responsibility for child care or domestic labour sets limits to her involvement in 'projects' and 'exploits'. There seem to be conceptual reasons, too, for her greater proneness to Sartrean immanence. Sartrean transcendence, like its Hegelian predecessor, is precisely a transcendence of 'life'. Man transcends species life; he 'creates values'.

> The female, to a greater extent than the male, is the prey of the species; and the human race has always sought to escape

its specific destiny. The support of life became for man an activity and a project through the invention of the tool; but in maternity woman remained closely bound to her body, like an animal. It is because humanity calls itself in question in the matter of living – that is to say, values the reasons for living above mere life – that, confronting woman, man assumes mastery. Man's design is not to repeat himself in time: it is to take control of the instant and mould the future. It is male activity that in creating values has made of existence itself a value; this activity has prevailed over the confused forces of life; it has subdued Nature and Woman.[16]

'Transcendence', in its origins, is a transcendence *of* the feminine. In its Hegelian version, this is a matter of breaking away from the nether world of women. In its Sartrean version, it is associated with a repudiation of what is supposedly signified by the female body, the 'holes' and 'slime' which threaten to engulf free subjecthood.[17] It is as if, in the lack of a Hegelian nether world, all that is left for subjecthood to transcend is the female body itself. In both cases, of course, it is only from a male perspective that the feminine can be seen as what must be transcended. But the male perspective has left its marks on the very concepts of 'transcendence' and 'immanence'. Perhaps it is not, after all, surprising that de Beauvoir should slip into those disconcerting passages where it seems that women must struggle not only with their own bad faith and male power, but with their own bodies, if they are to achieve true selfhood and freedom; as if they can achieve transcendence only at the expense of alienation from their bodily being.

What I am suggesting here is that the ideal of transcendence is, in a more fundamental way than de Beauvoir allows, a male ideal; that it feeds on the exclusion of the feminine. This is what makes the ideal of a feminine attainment of transcendence paradoxical. In Hegel's original version of the transcendence of life, women were outside the drama, relegated to a nether world. In de Beauvoir's application of the model, mediated through Sartre, women are fitted into the conflict of hostile consciousnesses; her ideal is that they struggle to become lookers, rather than always the looked-at. But can 'transcendence' be taken over in this way, as if it were a gender-neutral ideal? And what would remain of it in the lack of that Hegelian middle ground which Sartre and de Beauvoir would have us repudiate as a zone of bad faith? Male transcendence, as Hegel himself partly saw, is different from what female transcendence would have to be. It is breaking away from a zone which, for the male, remains intact – from what is for him the realm of particularity and merely natural feelings. For the female, in contrast, there is no such realm which she can both leave and leave intact.

7

Concluding remarks

What exactly does the 'maleness' of Reason amount to? It is clear that what we have in the history of philosophical thought is no mere succession of surface misogynist attitudes, which can now be shed, while leaving intact the deeper structures of our ideals of Reason. There is more at stake than the fact that past philosophers believed there to be flaws in female character. Many of them did indeed believe that women are less rational than men; and they have formulated their ideals of rationality with male paradigms in mind. But the maleness of Reason goes deeper than this. Our ideas and ideals of maleness and femaleness have been formed within structures of dominance – of superiority and inferiority, 'norms' and 'difference', 'positive' and 'negative', the 'essential' and the 'complementary'. And the male–female distinction itself has operated not as a straightfor-wardly descriptive principle of classification, but as an expression of values. We have seen that the equation of maleness with superiority goes back at least as far as the

Pythagoreans. What is valued – whether it be odd as against even numbers, 'aggressive' as against 'nurturing' skills and capacities, or Reason as against emotion – has been readily identified with maleness. Within the context of this association of maleness with preferred traits, it is not just incidental to the feminine that female traits have been construed as inferior – or, more subtly, as 'complementary' – to male norms of human excellence. Rationality has been conceived as transcendence of the feminine; and the 'feminine' itself has been partly constituted by its occurrence within this structure.

It is a natural response to the discovery of unfair discrimination to affirm the positive value of what has been downgraded. But with the kind of bias we are confronting here the situation is complicated by the fact that femininity, as we have it, has been partly formed by relation to, and differentiation from, a male norm. We may, for example, want to insist against past philosophers that the sexes are equal in possession of Reason; and that women must now be admitted to full participation in its cultural manifestations. But, as we have seen in the case of de Beauvoir's feminist appropriation of the ideal of transcendence, this approach is fraught with difficulty. Women cannot easily be accommodated into a cultural ideal which has defined itself in opposition to the feminine. To affirm women's equal possession of rational traits, and their right of access to the public spaces within which they are cultivated and manifested, is politically important. But it does not get to the heart of the conceptual complexities of gender difference. And in repudiating one kind of exclusion, de Beauvoir's mode of response can help reinforce another. For it seems implicitly to accept the downgrading of the excluded character traits traditionally associated with femininity, and to endorse the assumption that the only human excellences and virtues which deserve to be taken seriously are those exemplified in the range of activities and concerns that have been associated with maleness.

However, alternative responses are no less beset by conceptual complexities. For example, it may seem easy to affirm the value and strengths of distinctively 'feminine' traits without subscribing to any covertly assumed 'norm' – to have, as it were, a genuine version of Rousseau's idea that the female mind is equal, but different. But extricating concepts of femininity from the intellectual structures within which our understanding of sexual difference has been formed is more difficult than it seems. The idea that women have their own distinctive kind of intellectual or moral character has itself been partly formed within the philosophical tradition to which it may now appear to be a reaction. Unless the structural features of our concepts of gender are understood, any emphasis on a supposedly distinctive style of thought or morality is liable to be caught up in a deeper, older structure of male norms and female complementation. The affirmation of the value and importance of 'the feminine' cannot of itself be expected to shake the underlying normative structures, for, ironically, it will occur in a space already prepared for it by the intellectual tradition it seeks to reject.

Thus it is an understandable reaction to the polarizations of Kantian ethics to want to stress the moral value of 'feminine' concerns with the personal and particular, as against the universal and impartial; or the warmth of feeling as against the chillingly abstract character of Reason. But it is important to be aware that the 'exclusion' of the feminine has not been a straightforward repudiation. Subtle accommodations have been incorporated into the social organization of sexual division – based on, or rationalized by, philosophical thought – which allow 'feminine' traits and activities to be both preserved and downgraded. There has been no lack of male affirmation of the importance and attractiveness of 'feminine' traits – in women – or of gallant acknowledgement of the impoverishment of male Reason. Making good the lacks in male consciousness, providing it with a necessary complementation by the 'feminine', is a large part of what the suppression, and the correlative constitution, of 'womankind' has been all about. An affirmation of the strengths of female 'difference' which is unaware of this may be doomed to repeat some of the sadder subplots in the history of western thought.

The content of femininity, as we have it, no less than its subordinate status, has been formed within an intellectual tradition. What has happened has been not a simple exclusion of women, but a constitution of femininity through that exclusion. It is remarkable that Hegel, the notorious exponent of the 'nether world' of femininity, should have had such insight into the conceptual complexities of sexual difference. Hegel's diagnosis of 'womankind', as we have seen, occurs in a wider framework, which endorses the relegation of women to the private domain. But his understanding of the complexity, and the pathos, of gender difference in some ways transcends that. He saw that life in the nether world has conditioned the modes of female consciousness; that the distinctively 'feminine' is not a brute fact, but a structure largely constituted through suppression. To agree with this is not to deny that the 'feminine' has its own strengths and virtues. In the current climate of critical reflection on ideals of Reason, some of the strengths of female 'difference' can be seen as deriving from their very exclusion from 'male' thought-styles. To have been largely excluded from the dominant, and supposedly more 'advanced', forms of abstract thought or moral consciousness can be seen as a source of strength when their defects and impoverishment become apparent. But such strengths must be seen in relation to structural features of gender difference. They are strengths that derive from exclusion; and the merits of such 'minority consciousness' depend on avoiding asserting it as a rival norm.[1]

Attempting to identify or affirm anything distinctively 'feminine' has its hazards in a context of actual inequality. If the full range of human activities – both the nurturing tasks traditionally associated with the private domain and the activities which have hitherto occupied public space – were freely available to all, the exploration of sexual difference would be less fraught with the dangers of perpetuating norms and stereotypes which have mutilated men and women alike. But the task of exposing and criticizing the maleness of ideals of Reason need not wait upon the realization of such hopes; it may indeed be an important contribution to their realization.

The denigration of the 'feminine' is to feminists, understandably, the most salient aspect of the maleness of the philosophical tradition. But the issue is important for men, too. The lives of women incorporate the impoverishing restraints of Reason's transcended 'nether world'. But maleness, as we have inherited it, enacts, no less, the impoverishment and vulnerability of 'public' Reason. Understanding the contribution of past thought to 'male' and 'female' consciousnesses, as we now have them, can help make available a diversity of intellectual styles and characters to men and women alike. It need not involve a denial of all difference. Contemporary consciousness, male or female, reflects past philosophical ideals as well as past differences in the social organization of the lives of men and women. Such differences do not have to be taken as norms; and understanding them can be a source of richness and diversity in a human life whose full range of possibilities and experience is freely accessible to both men and women.

Can anything be salvaged of the ideal of a Reason which knows no sex? Much of past exultation in that ideal can be seen as a self-deceiving failure to acknowledge the differences between male and female minds, produced and played out in a social context of real inequalities. But it can also be seen as embodying a hope for the future. A similar ambiguity characterizes Hegel's own famous expression of faith in Reason, summed up in his slogan that the real is the rational and the rational the real. This has, not surprisingly, been seen by many as a dubious rationalization of the status quo. But it can also be taken as the expression of an ideal – as an affirmation of faith that the irrational will not prevail. Such a faith may well appear naive; but that does not mean it is bad faith. The confident affirmation that Reason 'knows no sex' may likewise be taking for reality something which, if valid at all, is so only as an ideal. Ideal equalities, here as elsewhere, can conceal actual inequalities. Notwithstanding many philosophers' hopes and aspirations to the contrary, our ideals of Reason are in fact male; and if there is a Reason genuinely common to all, it is something to be achieved in the future, not celebrated in the present. Past ideals of Reason, far from transcending sexual difference, have helped to constitute it. That ideas of maleness have developed under the guise of supposedly neutral ideals of Reason has been to the disadvantage of women and men alike.

Philosophers have defined their activity in terms of the pursuit of Reason, free of the conditioning effects of historical circumstance and social structures. But despite its professed transcendence of such contingencies, Philosophy has been deeply affected by, as well as deeply affecting, the social organization of sexual difference. The full dimensions of the maleness of Philosophy's past are only now becoming visible. Despite its aspirations to timeless truth, the History of Philosophy reflects the characteristic preoccupations and self-perceptions of the kinds of people who have at any time had access to the activity. Philosophers have at different periods been churchmen, men of letters, university professors. But there is one thing they have had in common throughout the history of the activity: they have been predominantly male; and the absence of women from the philosophical tradition has meant that the conceptualization of Reason has been done exclusively by men. It is not surprising that the results should reflect their sense of Philosophy as a male activity. There have of course been female philosophers throughout the western tradition. But, like Philo's or Augustine's women of Reason, they have been philosophers despite, rather than because of, their femaleness; there has been no input of femaleness into the formation of ideals of Reason.

As women begin to develop a presence in Philosophy, it is only to be expected that the maleness of Philosophy's past, and with it the maleness of ideals of Reason, should begin to come into focus; and that this should be accompanied by a sense of antagonism between feminism and Philosophy. We have seen that Philosophy has powerfully contributed to the exclusion of the feminine from cultural ideals, in ways that cannot be dismissed as minor aberrations of the philosophical imagination. But it is important that the tensions between feminism and Philosophy should not be misconstrued. The exclusion of the feminine has not resulted from a conspiracy by male philosophers. We have seen that in some cases it happened despite the conscious intent of the authors. Where it does appear explicitly in the texts, it is usually incidental to their main purposes; and often it emerges only in the conjunction of the text with surrounding social structures – a configuration which often is visible only in retrospect.

Feminist unease about ideals of Reason is sometimes expressed as a repudiation of allegedly male principles of rational thought. Such formulations of the point make it all too easy for professional philosophers to dismiss as confused all talk of the maleness of Reason. As I pointed out at the beginning, contemporary philosophical preoccupation with the requirements of rational belief, the objectivity of truth and the procedures of rational argument, can make it difficult for them to see the import of criticisms of broader cultural ideals associated with Reason. The claim that Reason is male need not at all involve sexual relativism about truth, or any suggestion that principles of logical thought valid for men do not hold also for female reasoners.

Philosophers can take seriously feminist dissatisfaction with the maleness of Reason without repudiating either Reason or Philosophy. Such criticisms of ideals of Reason can in fact be seen as continuous with a very old strand in the western philosophical tradition; it has been centrally concerned with bringing to reflective awareness the deeper structures of inherited ideals of Reason. Philosophy has defined ideals of Reason through exclusions of the feminine. But it also contains within it the resources for critical reflection on those ideals and on its own aspirations. Fortunately, Philosophy is not necessarily what it has in the past proudly claimed to be – a timeless rational representation of the real, free of the conditioning effects of history.

To study the History of Philosophy can be of itself to engage in a form of cultural critique. Few today share Hegel's vision of the History of Philosophy as the steady path of Reason's progress through human history. But it does reveal a succession of ways of construing Reason which have, for better or worse, had a formative influence on cultural ideals, and which still surface in contemporary consciousness. I have tried to bring out how these views of Reason have been connected with the male–female distinction. In doing so, I have of course often highlighted points which were not salient in the philosophers' own perceptions of what they were about. Bringing the male–female distinction to the centre of consideration of texts in this way may seem to misrepresent the History of Philosophy. But philosophers, when they tell the story of Philosophy's past, have always done so from the perspective of their own preoccupations, shared with their non-philosopher contemporaries – pressing questions which were not central to the philosophers they were explicating.

To highlight the male–female distinction in relation to philosophical texts is not to distort the History of Philosophy. It does, however, involve taking seriously the temporal distance that separates us from past thinkers. Taking temporal distance seriously demands also of course that we keep firmly in view what the thinkers themselves saw as central to their projects. This exercise involves a constant tension between the need to confront past ideals with perspectives drawn from the present and, on the other hand, an equally strong demand to present fairly what the authors took themselves to be doing. A constructive resolution of the tensions between contemporary feminism and past Philosophy requires that we do justice to both demands.

Notes

1 Reason, science and the domination of matter

INTRODUCTION

1 de Beauvoir, S. (1949) *The Second Sex*, trans. H.M. Parshley, Harmondsworth, Penguin Books, 1972, p. 97.
2 Nietzsche, F. (1871) 'The Greek woman', trans. M.A. Mügge, in Levy, O. (ed.) (1911) *The Complete Works of Friedrich Nietzsche*, vol. II, London, T.N. Foulis, pp. 22–3.

FEMININITY AND GREEK THEORIES OF KNOWLEDGE

3 Plato, *Menexenus*, 238a.
4 For a discussion of the symbolic significance in Greek literature of the succession of cults at Delphi, see Harrison, J. (1912) *Themis: A Study of the Social Origins of Greek Religion*, Cambridge, Cambridge University Press, pp. 385–96.

5 Aeschylus, *Eumenides*, 559, trans. G. Murray, in *The Complete Plays of Aeschylus*, London, Allen & Unwin, 1952, p. 235.

6 Plato, *Timaeus*, 50d.

7 Aristotle, *Metaphysics*, I, ch. 6, 998a 1–10, trans. R. McKeon, in *The Basic Works of Aristotle*, New York, Random House, 1941, p. 702.

8 Plato, *Timaeus*, 51e, trans. B. Jowett, in *The Dialogues of Plato*, vol. II, New York, Random House, 1937, p. 32.

9 Plato, *Phaedo*. Quotations are from the translation by F.J. Church, in *The Trial and Death of Socrates*, London, Macmillan, 1952.

10 Aristotle, op. cit., I, chs 6–10, in McKeon, op. cit., pp. 700–12.

11 Aquinas, T. (1267–73) *Summa Theologica*, I, Q.84, art. 1, trans. Fathers of the English Dominican Province, London, Burns, Oates & Washbourne, 1922, vol. IV, pp. 157–60.

FRANCIS BACON: KNOWLEDGE AS THE SUBJUGATION OF NATURE

12 Bacon, F. (1605) *The Advancement of Learning*, III, ch. 4, in Devey, J. (ed.) (1901) *The Physical and Metaphysical Works of Lord Bacon*, London, George Bell, p. 138.

13 Bacon, F. (1620a) *Novum Organum*, I, aphorism LI, in Devey, op. cit., p. 395.

14 Bacon, F. (1620b) *The Great Instauration*, 'Distribution of the work', in Devey, op. cit., p. 15.

15 Bacon (1605), op. cit., V, ch. 2, in Devey, op. cit., p. 188.

16 ibid., V, ch. 4, in Devey, op. cit., p. 207.

17 Bacon, F., *The Refutation of Philosophies*, trans. B. Farrington, in *The Philosophy of Francis Bacon: An essay on its development from 1603 to 1609 with new translations of fundamental texts*, Liverpool, Liverpool University Press, 1964, p. 131.

18 Bacon (1620a), op. cit., aphorism CXXIX, in Devey, op. cit., p. 447.

19 Bacon, F., *Thoughts and Conclusions*, in Farrington, op. cit., p. 99.

20 Bacon (1620b), op. cit., 'Announcement of the author', in Devey, op. cit., p. 1.

21 ibid., 'Distribution of the work', in Devey, op. cit., p. 16.

22 Bacon, F. (1653) *The Masculine Birth of Time*, ch. 1, in Farrington, op. cit., p. 62.

23 ibid., ch. 2, in Farrington, op. cit., p. 72.

24 Bacon (1620a), op. cit., I, aphorism CXXI, in Devey, op. cit., p. 441.

25 Bacon, *Thoughts and Conclusions*, sec. 13, in Farrington, op. cit., p. 83.

26 Bacon (1620b), op. cit., Preface, in Devey, op. cit., p. 3.

27 ibid., 'Distribution of the work', in Devey, op. cit., p. 20.

28 Bacon (1605), op. cit., III, ch. 3, in Devey, op. cit., pp. 122–3.

29 ibid., III, ch. 4, in Devey, op. cit., p. 140.

30 Bacon (1620a), op. cit., I, aphorism CXXI, in Devey, op. cit., p. 440.

31 ibid., II, aphorism IV, in Devey, op. cit., p. 451.

32 ibid., I, aphorism XCV, in Devey, op. cit., p. 427.

33 Bacon, *Thoughts and Conclusions*, sec. 16, in Farrington, op. cit., p. 93.

34 Bacon (1620a), op. cit., I, aphorism CXXIX, in Devey, op. cit., p. 446.

35 Bacon, *The Refutation of Philosophies*, in Farrington, op. cit., p. 129.

36 ibid., in Farrington, op. cit., p. 120.

37 Bacon, F. (1622–3) Preface to *The History of the Winds*, in Bacon, F., *Works*, vol. II, collected and edited by J. Spedding, R.L. Ellis and D.D. Heath, London, Longman, 1858–74, pp. 14–15; in Farrington, op. cit., pp. 54–5.

2 The divided soul: manliness and effeminacy

INTRODUCTION: PLATO ON REASON

1 Plato, *Republic*, 439–40, trans. B. Jowett, in *The Dialogues of*

Plato, vol. I, New York, Random House, 1937, pp. 703–4.

2   Plato, *Philebus*, 21e, in Jowett, op. cit., vol. II, pp. 353–4.

3   Quotations are from the translation by Jowett, op. cit., vol. I.

4   Plato, *Phaedrus*, 246a, in Jowett, op. cit., vol. I, p. 250.

5   Plato, *Symposium*, 205, in Jowett, op. cit., vol. I, p. 330.

PHILO: 'MANLY REASON' AND THE 'ENTANGLEMENTS' OF SENSE

6   See especially Philo, *Allegorical Interpretation of Genesis*, II, secs V–XIV, in *Philo*, vol. I, trans. F.H. Colson and G.H. Whitaker, Loeb Classical Library, London, Heinemann, 1929, pp. 233–57.

7   ibid., III, sec. LXXXIX, in Colson and Whitaker, op. cit., vol. I, p. 453.

8   ibid., II, sec. XVIII, in Colson and Whitaker, op. cit., vol. I, p. 271.

9   Philo, *On the Creation*, sec. LV, in Colson and Whitaker, op. cit., vol. I, p. 125.

10   ibid., sec. LIX, in Colson and Whitaker, op. cit., vol. I, p. 131.

11   ibid., sec. LIII, in Colson and Whitaker, op. cit., vol. I, p. 121.

12   Philo, *Allegorical Interpretation of Genesis*, sec. XIV, in Colson and Whitaker, op. cit., vol. I, pp. 255–6.

13   ibid., sec. X, in Colson and Whitaker, op. cit., vol. I, p. 249.

14   ibid., sec. XXIV, in Colson and Whitaker, op. cit., vol. I, p. 287.

15   Philo, *Special Laws*, III, sec. XXXII, in op. cit., vol. VII, p. 587.

16   For an extended treatment of Philo's use of male–female symbolism, see Baer, R.A. (1970) *Philo's Use of the Categories Male and Female*, Leiden, E.J. Brill.

17   Philo, *Allegorical Interpretation of Genesis*, III, sec. IV, in Colson and Whitaker, op. cit., vol. I, p. 307.

18 Philo, *Questions and Answers on Exodus*, I, sec. 8, trans. R. Marcus, in *Philo*, Loeb Classical Library, supplementary vol. II, pp. 15–16.

19 Philo, *That the Worse is Wont to Attack the Better*, sec. IX, in Colson and Whitaker, op. cit., vol. II, p. 221.

20 Philo, *On the Cherubim and the Flaming Sword*, sec. XIV, in Colson and Whitaker, op. cit., vol. II, p. 39.

21 Philo, *Special Laws*, I, sec. XXXVII, in Colson and Whitaker, op. cit., vol. VII, p. 215.

22 Philo, *Allegorical Interpretation of Genesis*, III, sec. LXXI, in Colson and Whitaker, op. cit., vol. I, p. 439.

23 Philo, *On the Creation*, sec. LVI, in Colson and Whitaker, op. cit., vol. I, p. 125.

AUGUSTINE: SPIRITUAL EQUALITY AND NATURAL SUBORDINATION

24 See especially, Augustine, *Confessions*, XIII, chs 32 and 34, trans. V.J. Bourke, in *The Fathers of the Church: A New Translation*, vol. XXI, Washington, The Catholic University of America Press, 1953; and *The Trinity*, XII, trans. S. McKenna, in *The Fathers of the Church: A New Translation*, vol. XLV, Washington, The Catholic University of America Press, 1963.

25 Augustine, *Confessions*, XIII, ch. 32, in Bourke, op. cit., p. 452.

26 Augustine, *De Trinitate*, XII, ch. 3, in McKenna, op. cit., p. 345.

27 ibid., XII, ch. 7, in McKenna, op. cit., pp. 351–5.

28 ibid., in McKenna, op. cit., p. 355.

29 ibid., XII, ch. 8, in McKenna, op. cit., p. 355.

30 ibid., X, ch. 8, in McKenna, op. cit., p. 305.

31 Augustine, *City of God*, XIV, ch. 23, trans. G.G. Walsh and G. Monahan, in *The Fathers of the Church: A New Translation*, vol. XIV, Washington, The Catholic University of America Press, 1952, p. 401.

32 Augustine, *On Continence*, ch. 9, sec. 23, trans. Sr M.F.

McDonald, 'Treatises on various subjects', in *The Fathers of the Church: A New Translation*, vol. XVI, Washington, The Catholic University of America Press, 1952, pp. 215–18.

AQUINAS: 'THE PRINCIPLE OF THE HUMAN RACE' AND HIS 'HELPMATE'

33 Aquinas, *Summa Theologica*, I, Q.76, art. 4, trans. Fathers of the English Dominican Province, London, Burns, Oates & Washbourne, 1922, vol. IV, pp. 39–43.

34 ibid., I, Q.92, art. 2, vol. IV, p. 277.

35 ibid., I, Q.93, art. 4, reply to obj. 1, vol. IV, p. 289.

36 ibid., I, Q.92, art. 1, vol. IV, p. 275.

37 ibid., p. 276.

38 ibid., II, Q.156, art. 1, vol. XIII, p. 173.

39 ibid., II, Q. 70, art. 3, vol. XI.

40 ibid., I, Q.92, art. 1, vol. IV, pp. 275–6.

3 Reason as attainment

INTRODUCTION

1 Hegel, G.W.F. (1821) *The Philosophy of Right*, trans. T.M. Knox, Oxford, Oxford University Press, 1952, add. 107, para. 166, pp. 263–4.

DESCARTES'S METHOD

2 Plato, *Phaedrus*, 270e. Quotations are from the translation by B. Jowett, in *The Dialogues of Plato*, vol. I, New York, Random House, 1937.

3 Descartes, R. (1701) *Rules for the Direction of the Mind*, rule IV, trans. E.S. Haldane and G.R.T. Ross, *The Philosophical Works of Descartes*, vol. I, Cambridge, Cambridge University Press, 1972, p. 9.

4 ibid.

5 ibid., rule I, in Haldane and Ross, op. cit., vol. I, pp. 1–2.

6 For an informative treatment of the contrasts between humanist pedagogical reforms and seventeenth-century versions of method, see Ong, W.J. (1958) *Ramus: Method and the Decay of Dialogue, From the Art of Discourse to the Art of Reason*, Cambridge, Mass., Harvard University Press.

7 Descartes, R. (1637) *Discourse on Method*, pt I, in Haldane and Ross, op. cit., vol. I, p. 81.

8 Letter to Vatier, 22 February 1638; in Alquié, F. (1967) *Oeuvres Philosophiques de Descartes*, vol. II, Paris, Editions Garnier Frères, p. 27.

9 Descartes (1637), op. cit., pt VI, in Haldane and Ross, op. cit., vol. I, p. 130.

10 For an interesting discussion of this aspect of the use of Latin, see Ong, W.J. (1971) 'Latin language study as a Renaissance puberty rite', in *Rhetoric, Romance and Technology: Studies in the Interaction of Expression and Culture*, Ithaca, NY, Cornell University Press.

11 Descartes (1701), op. cit., rule XII, in Haldane and Ross, op. cit., vol. I, p. 46.

12 ibid., rule VIII, in Haldane and Ross, op. cit., vol. I, p. 28.

13 Descartes, R. (1649) *The Passions of the Soul*, pt I, art. XLVII, in Haldane and Ross, op. cit., vol. I, p. 353.

14 Letter to Princess Elizabeth, 28 June 1643, in Kenny, A. (ed.) (1970) *Descartes: Philosophical Letters*, Oxford, Oxford University Press, pp. 140–3.

15 Descartes (1637), op. cit., pt I, in Haldane and Ross, op. cit., vol. I, 81–2.

16 ibid., pt VI, in Haldane and Ross, op. cit., vol. I, p. 120.

17 ibid., p. 119.

18 Princess Elizabeth to Descartes, 10/20 June 1643, trans. J. Blom, in *Descartes: His Moral Philosophy and Psychology*, Hassocks, Harvester Press, 1978, p. 111.

19 Letter to Princess Elizabeth, 28 June 1643, in Kenny, op. cit., pp. 140–3.

HUME ON REASON AND THE PASSIONS

20 Hume, D. (1734–6) *Treatise of Human Nature*, ed. L.A. Selby-Bigge, Oxford, Oxford University Press, 1960, vol. II, pt III, sec. III, p. 415.
21 ibid., vol. I, pt IV, sec. VII, p. 267.
22 ibid., p. 270.
23 ibid., vol. I, pt III, sec. III, pp. 414–15.
24 ibid., p. 416.
25 ibid., vol. III, pt I, sec. I, p. 458.
26 ibid., vol. II, pt III, sec. VIII, p. 438.
27 ibid., vol. III, pt II, sec. II, pp. 484–501.
28 ibid., p. 492.
29 ibid., vol. III, pt II, sec. VII, p. 536.
30 ibid., p. 538.

4   Reason and progress

INTRODUCTION

1 de Condorcet, A.-N. (1794) *Sketch of the Progress of the Human Mind*, in Gay, P. (ed.) (1973) *The Enlightenment: A Comprehensive Anthology*, New York, Simon & Schuster, p. 810.

ROUSSEAU: THE LOST YOUTH OF THE WORLD

2 Rousseau, J.J. (1750) *Discourse on the Moral Effects of the Arts and Sciences*, trans. G.D.H. Cole, in *The Social Contract and Discourses*, London, Dent, 1973, p. 25.
3 ibid., p. 26.
4 ibid., p. 13.
5 ibid., p. 18.
6 Rousseau, J.J. (1755) *Discourse on the Origin of Inequality*, in Cole, op. cit., p. 81.
7 ibid., p. 112.

8 Rousseau, J.J. (1762) *Social Contract*, I, ch. VIII, in Cole, op. cit., pp. 177–8.

9 Rousseau (1755), op. cit., in Cole, op. cit., p. 38.

10 ibid., p. 46.

11 Rousseau (1750) op. cit., in Cole, op. cit., p. 6.

12 Rousseau, J.J. (1761) *Julie or the New Héloise*, letter XI to Lord Bromston, trans. J.H. McDowell, University Park, Pa, Pennsylvania State University Press, 1968.

13 Rousseau, J.J. (1758) *Letter to d'Alembert*, trans. A. Bloom, as *Politics and the Arts*, Glencoe, Ill., Free Press, 1960, ch. VIII, p. 109.

14 Rousseau (1755), op. cit., in Cole, op. cit., p. 36.

KANT: FROM IMMATURITY TO ENLIGHTENMENT

15 In Reiss, H. (ed.) (1977) *Kant's Political Writings*, Cambridge, Cambridge University Press, pp. 41–53.

16 ibid., p. 41.

17 ibid., p. 44.

18 ibid., p. 45.

19 ibid., p. 49.

20 Kant, I. (1784) 'An answer to the question: "What is Enlightenment?"' in Reiss, op. cit., pp. 54–60.

21 Freud, S. (1925) 'Some psychical consequences of the anatomical distinction between the sexes', in Strachey, J. (ed.) (1966–74) *The Standard Edition of the Complete Psychological Works of Sigmund Freud*, vol. XIX, London, Hogarth Press, pp. 257–8.

HEGEL: REASON AS THE UNFOLDING OF NATURE

22 Rousseau (1762), op. cit., I, ch. VIII, in Cole, op. cit., p. 178.

23 Hegel, G.W.F. (1807) *Phenomenology of Spirit*, sec. 438, trans. A.V. Miller, Oxford, Oxford University Press, 1977, p. 263.

24 ibid., secs 206–30, pp. 126–38.
25 ibid., sec. 537, p. 328.
26 ibid., sec. 524, p. 319.

5   The public and the private

INTRODUCTION: COMPLEMENTARY CONSCIOUSNESSES

1 Rousseau, J.J. (1762) *Emile*, trans. B. Foxley, London, Dent, 1911, vol. V, pp. 321–2.
2 ibid., p. 349.
3 Kant, I. (1763) *Observations on the Feeling of the Beautiful and Sublime*, trans. J.T. Goldthwait, Berkeley and Los Angeles, University of California Press, 1960, sec. 3, p. 78.
4 ibid., p. 95.
5 Wollstonecraft, M. (1792) *A Vindication of the Rights of Woman*, ed. M. Kramnick, Harmondsworth, Penguin Books, 1975, ch. 5, p. 187.
6 In Schopenhauer, A. (1851) *Essays and Aphorisms*, trans. R.J. Hollingdale, Harmondsworth, Penguin Books, 1970.
7 Hegel, G.W.F. (1807) *Phenomenology of Spirit*, trans. A.V. Miller, Oxford, Oxford University Press, 1977, p. 288.
8 Hume, D. (1741–2) 'Essay writing', in *Essays, Moral, Political and Literary*, Oxford, Oxford University Press, 1963, pp. 568–72.

HEGEL: THE FEMININE NETHER WORLD

9 Hegel, op. cit., secs 444–76, pp. 266–90.
10 ibid., sec. 451, p. 269.
11 ibid., sec. 457, pp. 274–5.
12 ibid., sec. 475, p. 288.
13 ibid., sec. 460, p. 276.
14 ibid., sec. 463, p. 278.
15 ibid., sec. 458, p. 275.

16 ibid., sec. 457, p. 274.
17 Hegel, G.W.F. (1821) *Philosophy of Right*, trans. T.M. Knox, Oxford, Oxford University Press, 1942, add. 107, para. 166, pp. 263–4.

6   The struggle for transcendence

INTRODUCTION

1 de Beauvoir, S. (1949) *The Second Sex*, trans. H.M. Parshley, Harmondsworth, Penguin Books, 1972, p. 174.
2 ibid., p. 29.

HEGEL: SELF-CONSCIOUSNESS AS ACHIEVEMENT

3 Hegel, G.W.F. (1807) *Phenomenology of Spirit*, trans. A.V. Miller, Oxford, Oxford University Press, 1977, secs 166–96, pp. 104–19.
4 ibid., sec. 177, pp. 110–11.
5 ibid., secs 194–6, pp. 117–19.
6 Sartre, J.-P. (1943) *Being and Nothingness*, trans. H.E. Barnes, London, Methuen, 1958, pt III, ch. 1.

SARTRE AND DE BEAUVOIR: WOMEN AND TRANSCENDENCE

7 ibid., pp. 252–302.
8 ibid., p. 268.
9 ibid., p. 237.

DE BEAUVOIR ON WOMAN AS OTHER

10 de Beauvoir, op. cit., p. 21.
11 ibid., pp. 28–9.
12 ibid., p. 61.
13 Sartre, op. cit., pt IV, ch. 2, sec. 3, pp. 600–15.

14 de Beauvoir, op. cit., Introduction, bk 2, p. 31.
15 ibid., pp. 96–7.
16 ibid., p. 97.
17 Sartre, op. cit., pp. 613–14.

7 Concluding remarks

1 The phrase 'minority consciousness' is from Deleuze, G.
(1978) 'Philosophie et minorité', *Critique*, 369, 154–5.

Bibliographical essay

The following anthologies give some indication of the scope of recent philosophical work on gender and feminist critique of the philosophical tradition: R. Baker and F. Elliston (eds), *Philosophy and Sex* (Buffalo, NY, Prometheus Books, 1975); C. Gould and M. Wartofsky (eds), *Women and Philosophy: Toward a Theory of Liberation* (New York, Perigree Books, 1976); M. Vetterling-Braggin, F. Elliston and J. English (eds), *Feminism and Philosophy* (Totowa, NJ, Littlefield Adams, 1977); J. English (ed.), *Sex Equality* (Englewood Cliffs, NJ, Prentice-Hall, 1977); S. Bishop and M. Weinzeig (eds), *Philosophy and Women* (Belmont, Wadsworth, 1979); L. Clark and L. Lange (eds), *The Sexism of Social and Political Theory: Women and Reproduction from Plato to Nietzsche* (Toronto, University of Toronto Press, 1979); M. Vetterling-Braggin (ed.), *'Femininity', 'Masculinity' and 'Androgyny': A Modern Philosophical Discussion* (Totowa, NJ, Littlefield Adams, 1982); M. Vetterling-Braggin (ed.), *Sexist Language: A Modern Philosophical Analysis* (Totowa, NJ,

Littlefield Adams, 1982); C. Gould (ed.), *Beyond Domination: New Perspectives on Women and Philosophy* (Totowa, NJ, Littlefield Adams, 1983); S. Harding and M. Hintikka (eds), *Discovering Reality: Feminist Perspectives on Epistemology, Metaphysics, Methodology and the Philosophy of Science* (Dordrecht, Reidel, 1983).

The Monist has a special issue, 'Women's liberation: ethical, social and political issues', 57 (1) (January 1973); and *Radical Philosophy* also has a special issue, 'Women, gender and philosophy', 34 (Summer 1983). See also Jane English's review essay, 'Philosophy', in *Signs*, 3 (4) (Summer 1978), 823–31; and N.G. Keohane, 'Feminist scholarship and human nature', *Ethics*, 93 (1) (October 1982), 102–13.

Much of the work included in these collections is concerned with philosophical aspects of contemporary moral, political and social issues: abortion, sexual equality, affirmative action and preferential hiring, sexist language, sex roles. Articles devoted to feminist critique of the western philosophical tradition will be found especially in Clark and Lange (eds), *The Sexism of Social and Political Theory* and Harding and Hintikka (eds), *Discovering Reality*. Extensive critiques of the western political tradition from feminist perspectives have been offered in two books by political theorists. Susan M. Okin's book, *Women in Western Political Thought* (Princeton, NJ, Princeton University Press, 1979), discusses the treatment of women in the thought of Plato, Aristotle, Rousseau and Mill. Jean B. Elshtain's *Public Man, Private Woman: Women in Social and Political Thought* (Princeton, NJ, Princeton University Press, 1981) is a critique of the operations of the public–private distinction in relation to women, covering Plato, Aristotle, Augustine, Aquinas, Luther, Machiavelli, Hobbes, Locke and the liberal tradition, Rousseau, Hegel and Marx, and includes a survey of feminist attitudes to the public–private distinction and an attempted reconstruction of it. See also Okin's 'Women and the making of the sentimental family', *Philosophy and Public Affairs*, 11 (1), (Winter 1982), 65–88; and Elshtain's 'Feminist discourse and its discontents: language, power and meaning', *Signs*, 7 (3) (Spring 1982), 603–21. Mary O'Brien's book, *The Politics of*

Reproduction (London, Routledge & Kegan Paul, 1981), is also a critique of traditional political thought, focusing on conceptualizations of biological reproduction.

Two recent books have attempted to relate theories and techniques drawn from contemporary philosophy to the understanding and assessment of current feminist debate. Janet Radcliffe Richards's *The Skeptical Feminist: A Philosophical Enquiry* (Harmondsworth, Penguin Books, 1982) applies the techniques of analytical philosophy to restate feminist claims. Carol McMillan's *Women, Reason and Nature* (Oxford, Blackwell, 1982) uses a philosophical framework drawn from Wittgenstein and Winch in an assessment of contemporary feminism. She argues, from an explicitly anti-feminist perspective, that many feminists share dubious assumptions about rationality and human nature with philosophical rationalists. For an interesting discussion of the methodological issues raised by these two books, see the reviews by Jean Grimshaw of *The Skeptical Feminist*, in *Radical Philosophy*, 30 (Spring 1982), 1–6, and of *Women, Reason and Nature*, in *Radical Philosophy*, 34 (Summer 1983), 33–5; and the ensuing debate with Radcliffe Richards in *Radical Philosophy*, 32 (Autumn 1982), 42–3 and 34 (Summer 1983), 45–6.

In France, the male bias implicit in the philosophical tradition has been criticized by Luce Irigaray in *Speculum de l'autre femme* (Paris, Minuit, 1974), and *Ce sexe qui n'en est pas un* (Paris, Minuit, 1977). Irigaray is mainly concerned with the inapplicability to women of Freudian and Lacanian models of rationality. Michèle Le Doeuff, in *L'Imaginaire philosophique* (Paris, Payot, 1980), explores philosophers' use of imagery, including images of the feminine, and the implications of the ambivalent presence of women in the philosophical tradition. Two essays from Irigaray's *Ce sexe qui n'en est pas un* are translated in E. Marks and I. de Coutivron (eds), *New French Feminisms: An Anthology* (Amherst, Mass., University of Massachusetts Press, 1980). Two chapters from Le Doeuff's *L'Imaginaire philosophique* have been translated: 'Women and philosophy' ('Cheveux longs, idées courtes') in *Radical Philosophy*, 17 (Summer 1977), 2–11, and 'Pierre Roussel's chiasmas' in *Ideology and Consciousness*, 9 (Winter 1981/2), 39–70. Le Doeuff's work is discussed by Meaghan Morris in 'Operative reasoning: Michèle Le Doeuff, philosophy and feminism', *Ideology and Consciousness*, 9 (Winter 1981/2), 71–101.

The question of the cross-cultural universality of associations between femaleness and nature has received much attention from anthropologists. See specially S. Ortner, 'Is female to male as nature is to culture?' in M.Z. Rosaldo and L. Lamphere (eds), *Woman Culture and Society* (Stanford, Ca, Stanford University Press, 1974); E. Ardener, 'Belief and the problem of women', in J. La Fontaine (ed.), *The Interpretation of Ritual* (London, Tavistock, 1972) (also in S. Ardener (ed.), *Perceiving Women*, London, Malaby, 1975); C. MacCormack and M. Strathern (eds), *Nature, Culture and Gender* (Cambridge, Cambridge University Press, 1980).

The following is a selection of works dealing with treatments of gender by specific philosophers and intellectual movements discussed in this book.

On femininity in ancient thought, Raoul Mortley's *Womanhood: The Feminine in Ancient Hellenism, Gnosticism, Christianity and Islam* (Sydney, Delacroix, 1981) provides a useful survey. The transition from cults of the earth goddesses to religion associated with Reason in Greek thought, and its bearing on attitudes to the feminine, are discussed in the works of the classical archaeologist Jane Harrison: *Prologomena to the Study of Greek Religion* (Cambridge, Cambridge University Press, 1908); *Themis, a Study of the Social Origins of Greek Religion* (Cambridge, Cambridge University Press, 1912); and *Epilegomena to the Study of Greek Religion* (Cambridge, Cambridge University Press, 1921).

On Plato, the literature deals mainly with his treatment of equality of the sexes in Book V of the *Republic*; many of these sources, however, also discuss the implications for sexual difference of his theory of knowledge: C. Pierce, 'Equality: *Republic* V', *The Monist*, 57 (1) (1973), 1–11; C. Garside Allen, 'Plato on women', *Feminist Studies*, 2 (1975), 131–8; W. Fortenbaugh, 'On Plato's feminism in *Republic* V', *Apeiron*, 9 (1975), 1–4; M.L. Osborne, 'Plato's unchanging view of women: a denial that anatomy spells destiny', *The Philosophical Forum*, 6 (4) (1975), 447–52; A. Dickason, 'Anatomy and destiny: the role of biology in Plato's views of women', in Gould and Wartofsky (eds), *Women and Philosophy*, pp. 45–53; J. Annas, 'Plato's *Republic* and feminism', *Philosophy*, 51 (1976), 307–21; S.M. Okin, 'Philosopher queens and private wives: Plato on women and the family', *Philosophy and Public Affairs*, 6 (4) (1977), 345–69 (this article reappears in Okin's book, *Women in Western Political Thought*); H. Lesser, 'Plato's feminism', *Philosophy*, 54 (1979), 113–17; L. Lange, 'The function of equal education in Plato's *Republic* and *Laws* III', in Clark and Lange (eds), *The Sexism of Social and Political Theory*; J. Martin, 'Sex equality and education in Plato's Just State', in Vetterling-Braggin (ed.), *'Femininity', 'Masculinity' and 'Androgyny'*.

On Aristotle, the literature covers his theory of generation in the biological works and his treatment of the subordinate position of women: C. Garside Allen, 'Can a woman be good in the same way as a man?', *Dialogue*, 10 (1971), 534–44; P. Thom, 'Stiff cheese for women', *Philosophical Forum*, 8 (1) (1976), 94–107; W.W. Fortenbaugh, 'Aristotle on slaves and women', in J. Barnes, M. Schofield and R. Sorabji (eds), *Articles on Aristotle: 2, Ethics and Politics* (London, Duckworth, 1977), pp. 135–9; L. Lange, 'Woman is not a rational animal: on Aristotle's biology of reproduction', in Harding and Hintikka (eds), *Discovering Reality*, pp. 1-16.

Philo's use of sexual symbolism is extensively discussed in Richard A. Baer, *Philo's Use of the Categories Male and Female* (Leiden, E.J. Brill, 1970).

On attitudes to the feminine in the history of Christian thought, see Rosemary Ruether (ed.), *Religion and Sexism* (New York, Simon & Schuster, 1974). Two articles in that collection deal with the treatment of femaleness by Augustine and

Aquinas: Rosemary Ruether, 'Misogynism and virginal feminism in the Fathers of the Church', pp. 150–83, and Eleanor
McLaughlin, 'Equality of souls, inequality of sexes: woman in
mediaeval theology', pp. 213–66.

On Renaissance concepts of femininity, see I. Maclean, *The
Renaissance Notion of Woman: A Study in the Fortunes of Scholasticism
and Medical Science in European Intellectual Life* (Cambridge,
Cambridge University Press, 1980). Ruth Kelso's *Doctrine for the
Lady of the Renaissance* (Urbana, Ill., University of Illinois Press,
1956) is a useful source book on the education of Renaissance
noblewomen.

Carolyn Merchant's *The Death of Nature: Women, Ecology and
the Scientific Revolution* (San Francisco, Harper & Row, 1980),
explores the impact of the scientific revolution on attitudes to
women and nature.

Bacon's use of sexual metaphor and its implications for the
self-image of science are illuminatingly discussed in the work of
Evelyn Fox Keller: see especially 'Baconian science: a her-
maphroditic birth', *Philosophical Forum*, 11 (3) (1980), 299–308;
'Nature as "her"', *Proceedings of 'The Second Sex' Conference* (New
York University, 1979); 'Gender and science', *Psychoanalysis and
Contemporary Thought*, 1 (3) (1978), 409–33 (also in Harding and
Hintikka (eds), *Discovering Reality*, pp. 187–205); 'Feminism and
science', *Signs*, 7 (3) (1982), 589–602.

On the implications of Descartes's philosophy for sexual
difference, see G. Lloyd, 'The Man of Reason', *Metaphilosophy*,
10 (1979), 18–37; and J. Thompson, 'Women and the high
priests of Reason', *Radical Philosophy*, 34 (Summer 1983), 10–14.

Hume's brief remarks on sexual difference are discussed in S.
Burns, 'The Humean female', and L. Marcil-Lacoste, 'The
consistency of Hume's position concerning women', both in
Dialogue, 15(3) (1976), 414–24 and 425–40; and S. Burns and L.
Marcil-Lacoste, 'Hume on women', in Clark and Lange (eds),
The Sexism of Social and Political Theory, pp. 53–73. See also C.
Battersby, 'An enquiry concerning the Humean woman',
Philosophy, 56 (1981), 303–12.

On Rousseau, see E. Rapaport, 'On the future of love:
Rousseau and the radical feminists', *Philosophical Forum*, 5 (1–2)

(1973–4), 185–205 (also in Gould and Wartofsky (eds), *Women and Philosophy*, pp. 185–205); V.G. Wexler, '"Made for man's delight": Rousseau as anti-feminist', *American Historical Review*, 81 (1976), 266–91; L. Lange, 'Women and the general will', in Clark and Lange (eds), *The Sexism of Social and Political Theory*, pp. 41–52; C. Pateman, '"The disorder of women": women, love and the sense of justice', *Ethics*, 91 (1980), 20–34; M. Bloch and J.H. Bloch, 'Women and the dialectics of nature in eighteenth-century French thought', in MacCormack and Strathern (eds), *Nature, Culture and Gender*, pp. 25–41; J. Martin, 'Sophie and Emile: a case study of sex bias in the history of educational thought', *Harvard Educational Review*, 51(3) (1981), 357–72; G. Lloyd, 'Rousseau on Reason, Nature and women', *Metaphilosophy*, 14 (3/4) (July/October 1983), 308–26.

On Kant and Hegel, see L. Blum, 'Kant's and Hegel's moral rationalism – a feminist perspective', *Canadian Journal of Philosophy*, 12 (2) (1982), 287–302; and P.J. Mills, 'Hegel and "the woman question": recognition and intersubjectivity', in Clark and Lange (eds), *The Sexism of Social and Political Theory*, pp. 74–98.

Sartre's descriptions of the feminine in *Being and Nothingness* are discussed in M. Collins and C. Pierce, 'Holes and slime: sexism in Sartre's psychoanalysis', in Gould and Wartofsky (eds), *Women and Philosophy*, pp. 112–27; W. Barrett, *Irrational Man* (New York, Doubleday Anchor, 1962), pt III, ch. 10; and R. Keat, 'Masculinity in philosophy', *Radical Philosophy*, 34 (Summer 1983), 15–20.

De Beauvoir's treatment of female biology and her use of the Sartrean framework are discussed in D. Kaufman McCall, 'Simone de Beauvoir, *The Second Sex* and Jean-Paul Sartre', *Signs*, 5 (2) (Winter 1979), 209–23; Michèle Le Doeuff, 'Operative philosophy: Simone de Beauvoir and existentialism', *Ideology and Consciousness*, 6 (Autumn 1979), 47–58; B. Easlea, *Science and Sexual Oppression* (London, Weidenfeld & Nicholson, 1981), ch. 2; E. Spelman, 'Woman as body: ancient and contemporary views', *Feminist Studies*, 8 (1) (1982), 109–31.

The conceptual problems in identifying distinctive male and female traits and the relations between sex and gender are explored in the papers in Mary Vetterling-Braggin (ed.), *'Femininity', 'Masculinity' and 'Androgyny'*. Her earlier collection, *Feminism and Philosophy*, co-edited with F. Elliston and J. English, also includes a section on sex roles and gender which contains some of the articles reprinted in the later volume. Questions about the maleness of the styles and assumptions embodied in philosophical thought,and the ways in which gender may be reflected in theories of knowledge, are discussed in some of the papers in Harding and Hintikka (eds), *Discovering Reality*; and also in L. Code, 'Is the sex of the knower epistemologically significant?', *Metaphilosophy*, 12 (1981), 267–76; and R. Keat, 'Masculinity in philosophy', *Radical Philosophy*, 34 (Summer 1983), 15–20.

The question of different moral consciousness in men and women is interestingly discussed by the psychologist Carol Gilligan in 'In a different voice: women's conceptions of self and of morality', *Harvard Education Review*, 47 (4) (1977), 481–517; and in her book, *In a Different Voice* (Cambridge, Mass., Harvard University Press, 1982). Gilligan argues that women, rather than being less morally developed than men, as they are commonly taken to be (for example, in applications of Kohlberg's scale of moral development), should be seen as having their own kind of moral consciousness, grounded in a different mode of social experience and interpretation. Although Gilligan does not explore the conceptual complexities of distinctive 'male' and 'female' moral character, her work raises important questions about the Kantian equation of moral consciousness with the grasp of universal principles.

Much contemporary debate on feminist theory bears on the issues of 'difference' and 'norms' touched on in the concluding chapter of this book. The question of 'difference' has received a great deal of attention in current French feminist theory. See the papers included in H. Eisenstein and A. Jardine (eds), *The Future of Difference* (Boston, G.K. Hall, 1980); and in Marks and de Coutivron (eds), *New French Feminisms: An Anthology*. *Signs* has a special issue on French feminist theory – 7 (1) (Autumn 1981). The introduction to Eisenstein and Jardine's collection provides a useful discussion of changes in feminist attitudes to sexual difference.

The following is a guide to philosophical and other works which, although not centrally concerned with issues of gender, provide useful related reading on aspects of the history of philosophy covered in this book.

G.E.R. Lloyd, in *Polarity and Analogy: Two Types of Argumentation in Early Greek Thought* (Cambridge, Cambridge University Press, 1966), discusses the operations of 'polarities' in Greek thought; he includes some discussion of the male–female distinction in the Pythagorean table of opposites.

On early Greek attitudes to Reason and the location of the rational in relation to the non-rational in Greek thought, see E.R. Dodds, *The Greeks and the Irrational* (Berkeley, University of California Press, 1956) and *The Ancient Concept of Progress, and Other Essays on Greek Literature and Belief* (Oxford, Clarendon Press, 1973); and Bruno Snell, *The Discovery of the Mind, the Greek Origins of European Thought* (Oxford, Blackwell, 1953). K.J. Dover, in *Greek Homosexuality* (London, Duckworth, 1978), ch. 3, discusses the relations between philosophy and erotic love in Greek thought; see also G. Vlastos, 'The individual as an object of love in Plato', in *Platonic Studies* (Princeton, NJ, Princeton University Press, 1973), pp. 3–42, for a discussion of Greek accounts of love and friendship and their connections with philosophical thought.

On Bacon's treatment of knowledge, see B. Farrington, *The Philosophy of Francis Bacon: An essay on its development from 1603 to 1609, with new translations of fundamental texts* (Liverpool, Liverpool University Press, 1964); and L. Jardine, *Francis Bacon: Discovery and the Art of Discourse* (London, Cambridge University Press, 1975).

On Renaissance concepts of method, see N.W. Gilbert, *Renaissance Concepts of Method* (New York, Columbia University Press, 1960). On Descartes's method, see L.J. Beck, *The Method of Descartes: A Study of the Regulae* (Oxford, Oxford University Press, 1952). Walter J. Ong has an illuminating discussion of the contrasts between Renaissance concepts of method and their difference from later seventeenth-century versions of method in *Ramus: Method and the Decay of Dialogue, from the Art of Discourse to the Art of Reason* (Cambridge, Mass., Harvard University Press, 1958). See also his discussion of the significance of Latin as the language of the learned in 'Latin language study as a Renaissance puberty rite', in *Rhetoric, Romance and Technology: Studies in the Interaction of Expression and Culture* (Ithaca, NY, Cornell University Press, 1971).

The contrasts between the inertness of Humean instrumental Reason and Greek versions of Reason are discussed in Julia Annas's book, *An Introduction to Plato's Republic* (Oxford, Oxford University Press, 1981), ch. 5. The social and political significance of the account of reason and the passions exemplified by Hume are discussed in Albert O. Hirschman, *The Passions and the Interests: Arguments for Capitalism before its Triumph* (Princeton, NJ, Princeton University Press, 1977).

Lawrence A. Blum, in *Friendship, Altruism and Morality* (London, Routledge & Kegan Paul, 1980), raises questions about the Kantian treatment of the relations between Reason and emotion which bear on some of the points raised in my discussion of the 'Kantian' approach to ethics. See also Iris Murdoch's misgivings about Kantian ethics in *The Sovereignty of Good* (London, Routledge & Kegan Paul, 1970).

Some writings on Reason by contemporary English-speaking philosophers bear on the concerns of this book. Bryan Wilson (ed.), *Rationality* (Oxford, Blackwell, 1970), and S. Hollis and S. Lukes (eds) *Rationality and Relativism* (Oxford, Blackwell, 1982) are useful collections on relativism and its bearing on questions of the objectivity and universality of Reason. Hilary Putnam's *Reason, Truth and History* (Cambridge, Cambridge University Press, 1981) attempts an account of truth and rationality which undercuts the dichotomy between relativism and commitment to ahistorical, unchanging principles. And Richard Rorty, in *Philosophy and the Mirror of Nature* (Princeton, NJ, Princeton University Press, 1979) and *Consequences of Pragmatism* (Brighton, Harvester

Press, 1982), offers a broader critique of the traditional pretensions of philosophy to deliver timelessly true representations of reality, and of the associations between conceptions of reason and the understanding of truth as a correspondence between thought and reality.

However, the kinds of question I have raised about Reason have more affinities with some recent European philosophy, which has gone beyond the more narrowly epistemological concerns characteristic of much contemporary Anglo-Saxon philosophy's discussions of Reason. Philosophers of the Frankfurt school have explored the implications and consequences of Enlightenment ideals of Reason and progress. See especially the critique of instrumental reason and its implicit attitude to nature in T. Adorno and M. Horkheimer, *Dialectic of Enlightenment*, trans. J. Cumming (London, Verso, 1972); and M. Horkheimer, *The Eclipse of Reason* (New York, Oxford University Press, 1947; reprinted New York, Seabury Press, 1974); and the discussion of the 'interests' of Reason in J. Habermas, *Knowledge and Human Interest*, trans. J. Shapiro (Boston, Beacon Press, 1971). H.-G. Gadamer's *Reason in the Age of Science*, trans. F.G. Lawrence (Cambridge, Mass., MIT Press, 1981) also discusses the contrasts between contemporary accounts of, and attitudes to, Reason, and those of earlier thinkers.

The works of Michel Foucault also explore the contribution of past ideas of rationality, and the exclusion implicit in them, to the operations of norms and stereotypes. His *History of Sexuality*, vol. I, trans. Robert Hurley (New York, Random House, 1980) is particularly relevant to the questions raised in this book.

Index

acquisitiveness...
activity, 1, 7, 8, 9, 20, 21, 23
49, 57...
Aeschylus...
Aquinas, St. Thomas...
8, 9, 23, 51, 57...
Aristophanes...
31, 56, 90...
Augustine, St...
28, 56, 57...
autonomy...

Bacon, Francis...
18, 31, 56, 57, 58, 89, 90
bad faith, 97, 99, 100...
Beauvoir, Simone de...
86, 90, 91, 92, 93...
belief, xiii-xiv...
body, 5, 6, 11, 21, 31, 37, 39, 40
41, 42, 45, 70, 75, 76, 77...
29, 31, 90, 96...

chastity, 1-2, 3, 5, 7, 8, 9...

Index

acquisitiveness, 54–6, 79, 92

activity, 1–3, 14, 16, 24, 27, 41, 46–7, 49, 51, 74, 79, 81–3, 85, 101, 104–8

Aeschylus (524–456 BC), 2, 4

Aquinas, St Thomas (*c.*1225–74), 8–9, 22, 33–7, 75

Aristotle (384–322 BC), 4, 7–10, 13, 34, 36, 40–2, 51, 127

Augustine, St (AD 354–430), ix, 22, 28–36, 39, 46, 75, 108

autonomy, 44, 67, 71, 80, 87

Bacon, Francis (1561–1626), 7, 9–17, 48, 57, 59, 61–2, 128, 131

bad faith, 97–9, 101–2, 107

Beauvoir, Simone de (1908–   ), 1, 86–7, 92–102, 104, 129

belief, viii–x, 51–2, 109

body, 5–9, 12, 17–21, 24, 26, 29–34, 41–2, 45–7, 50, 78, 95, 99; female, 29–31, 99–101

chastity, 11–12, 15, 17

complementation, 29–31, 50, 74–6, 78, 87, 103–5

consciousness, 2, 50, 58, 67–8, 70, 71–2, 74, 80, 82–4, 87–99, 102, 105–7, 110, 130; ethical/moral, 67, 69, 70–1, 80, 83, 91, 106, 130; female, 38, 50, 70, 73, 77, 80, 82–4, 106–7; male, 50, 69, 73, 82–4, 105, 107; self-, 60, 70–1, 80–102; unhappy, 72

contemplation, 7–13, 20, 22, 30–2, 39, 46, 49

culture, viii–xi, 2, 16, 66, 99, 104, 109–10

death, 6, 77, 88–92, 95

Delphi, oracle of, 2–3, 111

Descartes, René (1596–1650), 39–52, 56–8, 69, 75, 78, 128, 131

difference, sexual, *see* sexual difference

Diotima, 21–2

dominance, 2, 5, 7, 9, 11–13, 16–19,

23, 27, 29, 46, 56, 92, 96, 103, 106
dualism, 5–6, 8, 19, 99; *see also* mind, relation to body

education, 43–4, 63, 76, 78, 100, 128
Elizabeth, Princess, 47–8
Enlightenment, 57–8, 64–8, 72, 133
equality, 28–9, 32–3, 44, 48–9, 59–63, 104, 106–7, 123–4, 126–8
Euripides (485–407 BC), 2
existentialism, 93, 95

family, 44, 56, 80–5, 91–2
feeling, 19, 61–2, 68–71, 76, 80–5, 91, 102, 105
femaleness, x, 2–3, 5, 11, 16–17, 22, 25–7, 31–2, 37, 39, 63, 73, 75, 79, 84, 86–7, 103–6, 108, 125–8
feminine, the, x, 2, 4, 16–17, 26, 31, 58, 64, 77, 80, 83–4, 87, 99–101, 104–9, 125–7, 129
feminism, x, 98, 104, 107–10, 123–5, 130
fertility, 2, 22
form-matter distinction, 3–5, 7–11, 16, 18, 34
forms, 4, 7, 8–11, 13–14, 16, 19–21, 34, 75
freedom, 6, 58, 67, 71, 81, 87, 93–8, 101
Freud, Sigmund (1856–1939), 69

gender, viii–x, 5, 24, 26–8, 37, 45, 72, 78, 91, 102, 104–6, 123, 126, 129–31
generation, 3, 21–2, 25, 33, 35–6, 127; *see also* Greek theory of generation
Genesis, 12, 22–4, 28–30, 35–7
God, 4, 6, 10, 15, 19, 23–31, 35–6, 43
goddesses, 2–3, 126
gods, 2, 5, 15, 20
Greek: influence on, and contrasts with, later thought, 7–11, 16–17, 22, 24, 28–9, 33–4, 39, 51, 75, 132; religion, 2–3, 6, 111, 126; theories of knowledge, 4–6, 10–11, 16–17, 131; theory of generation, 3, 127

happiness, 13, 21, 57–9, 82

Hegel, G.W.F. (1770–1831), 38, 58, 70–3, 77, 79, 81–5, 87–93, 98–102, 106–7, 109, 129
Hume, David (1711–76), 50–6, 68–9, 79, 128, 132
humility, 15

imagination, 46–8, 50, 52
immortality, 6, 21, 24
intellect, 6, 8, 9, 11, 16–17, 19, 30, 34, 45–7, 50, 62
intuition, 45, 68, 84

justice, 55–6, 60, 69

Kant, Immanuel (1724–1804), 51, 64–7, 69–72, 75–6, 80, 105, 129–30, 132
knowledge, ix, 2, 4, 5, 7–17, 19–21, 27, 38, 41, 43–5, 47–8, 50–2, 57–9, 61, 68, 131; scientific, 8, 10–11, 16, 58; *see also* theories of knowledge

labour, 14, 49–50, 76, 90–1, 93, 95, 100
law, 10, 65, 71, 80–1, 83–4, 88, 91
life, ix, 1, 4, 6, 19, 22–4, 27, 30, 33, 35, 38–9, 46–9, 51, 53–4, 60, 62, 65, 68–9, 74, 76–81, 87–93, 95–6, 99–101, 106–7; and death struggle, 89, 91–3, 96; ethical, 80–4, 88, 91–2, 98; Family, 79–83, 91–2; good, the, 19, 21, 24, 26
love, 19–22, 32, 40, 60, 66, 92

male-female distinction, 2–4, 7, 9, 11, 16–17, 22, 24–35, 38, 48, 50–1, 56, 58, 73, 75–9, 82–3, 91–3, 99–103, 105–6, 108, 110, 114, 129–31; associations with form-matter distinction, 3–5, 16, 22, 26; associations with mind-body distinction, 29–33; associations with morality, 24, 26–7, 51, 58, 63–4, 67, 69–70, 76–85, 98, 105, 130; associations with public-private distinction, 43–5, 56, 67, 70, 74, 77–9, 80–5, 87, 106–7, 124; associations with Reason-Nature distinction, 1–3, 11, 16, 58–9, 63–4, 78–9; as symbol

You still
haven't
learned how
to play?!

krak

Takeshi Obata

Not yet.
—Takeshi Obata

t all began when Yumi Hotta played a pick-up game of go with her father-in-law. As she was learning how to play, Ms. Hotta thought it might be fun to create a story around the traditional board game. More confident in her storytelling abilities than her drawing skills, she submitted the beginnings of **Hikaru no Go** to **Weekly Shonen Jump**'s Story King Award. The Story King Award is an award that picks the best story, manga, character design and youth (under 15) manga submissions every year in Japan. As fate would have it, Ms. Hotta's story (originally named, "**Kokonotsu no Hoshi**"), was a runner-up in the "Story" category of the Story King Award. Many years earlier, Takeshi Obata was a runner-up for the Tezuka Award, another Japanese manga contest sponsored by **Weekly Shonen Jump** and **Monthly Shonen Jump**. An editor assigned to Mr. Obata's artwork came upon Ms. Hotta's story and paired the two for a full-fledged manga about go. The rest is modern go history.

HIKARU NO GO VOL. 12
The SHONEN JUMP Manga Edition

This manga contains material that was originally published in English from
SHONEN JUMP #61 to #64. Artwork in the magazine may have been
slightly altered from that presented here.

STORY BY YUMI HOTTA
ART BY TAKESHI OBATA
Supervised by YUKARI UMEZAWA (5 Dan)

Translation & English Adaptation/Andy Nakatani
English Script Consultant/Janice Kim (3 Dan)
Touch-up Art & Lettering/Inori Fukuda Trant
Cover Design/Courtney Utt
Interior Design/Aaron Cruse
Additional Touch-up/Rachel Lightfoot
Editors/ Yuki Takagaki & Annette Roman

Editor in Chief, Books/Alvin Lu
Editor in Chief, Magazines/Marc Weidenbaum
VP of Publishing Licensing/Rika Inouye
VP of Sales/Gonzalo Ferreyra
Sr. VP of Marketing/Liza Coppola
Publisher/Hyoe Narita

Printed in the U.S.A.

Published by VIZ Media, LLC
P.O. Box 77010
San Francisco, CA 94107

SHONEN JUMP Manga Edition
10 9 8 7 6 5 4 3 2 1
First printing, May 2008

www.viz.com

THE WORLD'S
MOST POPULAR MANGA

www.shonenjump.com

Hikaru no Go

12 THE SHINSHODAN SERIES

STORY BY
YUMI HOTTA

ART BY
TAKESHI OBATA

Supervised by
YUKARI UMEZAWA
(5 Dan)

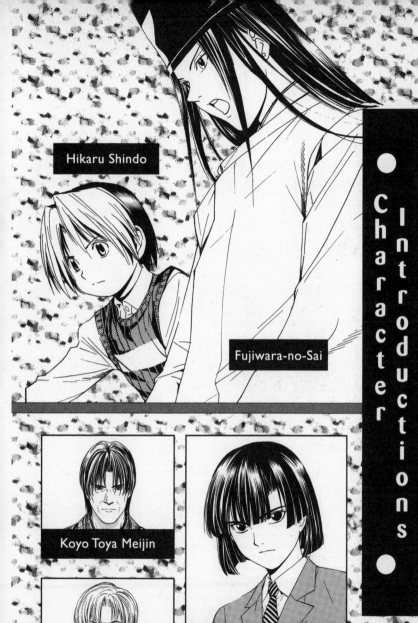

Hikaru Shindo

Fujiwara-no-Sai

Koyo Toya Meijin

Akira Toya

Ogata 9-dan

Character Introductions

Kuwabara Hon'inbo

Saeki

Kosuke Ochi

Shirakawa 7-dan

Zama Oza

Morishita 9-dan

Yoshitaka Waya

The Story Thus Far

Hikaru Shindo discovers an old go board one day up in his grandfather's attic. The moment Hikaru touches the board, the spirit of Fujiwara-no-Sai, a genius go player from Japan's Heian Era, enters his consciousness. Sai's love of go inspires Hikaru, as does a meeting with the child prodigy Akira Toya — son of go master Toya Meijin. With his interest in go awakened, Hikaru now dreams of becoming a professional player.

After the preliminary rounds of the pro test, Hikaru gains more experience and skill playing games at various go salons. The main rounds of the pro test are before him—and with 27 rounds to be played, only the top three players will move on to become pros. By the 25th round, Ochi has guaranteed his spot by maintaining his one-loss record. But the other two spots are up for grabs—and among the contenders are Waya with two losses, Hikaru with three, and Isumi and Honda both with four.

In round 26, Hikaru goes up against his rival Waya, and manages to come back from behind. Honda loses and thus eliminates his chance of going pro. In the final match, Hikaru goes up against Ochi, who has been receiving guidance from the younger Toya specifically aimed at defeating Hikaru. Hikaru, however, takes advantage of the slightest weakness in Ochi's game and manages to take the win. Waya also wins, which eliminates Isumi's hopes for a playoff. After 26 grueling rounds of play, Hikaru, Waya and Ochi have made it to the pros!

CONTENTS

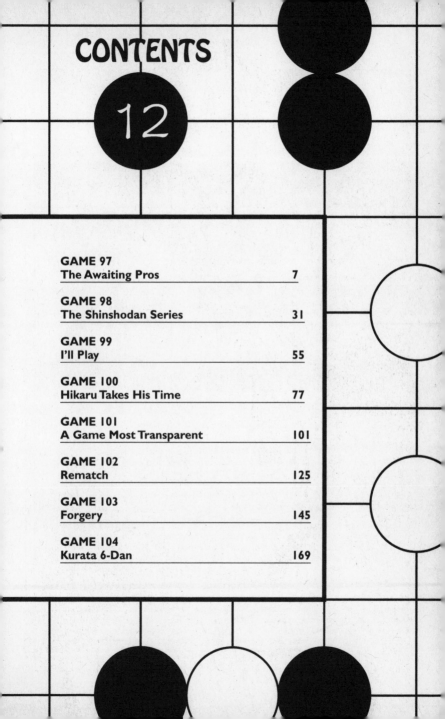

12

GAME 97
The Awaiting Pros   7

GAME 98
The Shinshodan Series   31

GAME 99
I'll Play   55

GAME 100
Hikaru Takes His Time   77

GAME 101
A Game Most Transparent   101

GAME 102
Rematch   125

GAME 103
Forgery   145

GAME 104
Kurata 6-Dan   169

Game 97 "The Awaiting Pros"

WHAT?! ISUMI QUIT THE KYUSEIKAI?

EVEN PEOPLE WHO PLAN TO MOVE ON USUALLY STICK AROUND UNTIL MARCH.

AND THAT'S NOT ALL. HE QUIT BEING AN INSEI.

DROPPING OUT OF THE INSEI AND THE KYUSEIKAI... WHAT'S HE GONNA DO? WAYA, HAVE YOU TALKED TO HIM?

BUT ISUMI'S BEEN GOING TO THE KYUSEIKAI FOR A REAL LONG TIME, RIGHT?!

THAT'S WHEN SHINODA SENSEI TOLD ME THAT ISUMI QUIT.

...SO I WENT TO THE GO ASSOCIATION ON AN INSEI GAME DAY.

WELL, I THOUGHT IT WOULD BE AWKWARD TO TALK TO HIM ON THE PHONE...

WHAT?!

SENSEI SAID THIS MIGHT BE BEST FOR ISUMI...

HE MAY HAVE DROPPED OUT FROM HERE AND THE KYUSEIKAI, BUT STUDYING GO ISN'T **JUST** ABOUT PLAYING GAMES.

PERHAPS THIS IS A TIME FOR QUIET INTROSPECTION...

AND AT **HIS** LEVEL, IT'S ENOUGH FOR HIM TO JUST REVIEW GAME RECORDS.

SOMETIMES IT'S A GOOD THING TO GO IT ALONE.

9

SENSEI SAID THAT ISUMI ISN'T DONE YET...

WHAT IF ISUMI GIVES UP FOREVER?!

WHAT THE HECK IS HE TALKING ABOUT?

HE SAID THAT ISUMI KNOWS THAT HE HASN'T TAKEN HIS GAME AS FAR AS IT CAN GO.

AND HE REALLY MEANT IT.

.....

HE SAID THAT FROM HERE ON OUT, I'LL HAVE TO WORK HARDER THAN I EVER HAVE BEFORE.

...TO KEEP MY NOSE OUT OF ISUMI'S BUSINESS.

THEN SENSEI TOLD ME...

ANYWAY, I THOUGHT I SHOULD TEACH YOU HOW TO BE A GAME RECORDER.

That goes for you too, Hikaru!

I GUESS THEY DON'T ASK KIDS WHO'RE STILL GOING TO SCHOOL, THOUGH...

SOME-TIMES YOU'LL GET ASKED TO DO IT.

A GAME RECORDER?

BUT I ALREADY KNOW HOW TO RECORD GAMES!

STARTING WITH THE THIRD ROUND OF PRELIMINARY MATCHES, ALL THE MOVES ARE RECORDED BY AN OFFICIAL GAME RECORDER.

YOU ALSO HAVE TO RECORD THE TIME.

SEE? LIKE THIS!

YOU HAVE TO RECORD HOW LONG EACH MOVE TOOK AND KEEP TRACK OF THE TOTAL TIME.

WHAT THE—?!

THEN THERE'S THE PERSON WHO COUNTS DOWN THE SECONDS IN OVERTIME.

I don't know if you're up to the task, Hikaru...

WHAT?!

HOW CAN YOU DO SOMETHING THIS HARD?

SURE.

WAYA—YOU CAN DO ALL THIS?

12

At last, Hikaru takes his first step into the professional world of go.

IT'S FOR YOUR OWN GOOD! I'M JUST TRYING TO HELP!

WHY'D YOU HAVE TO SHOW ME THIS?!

PLAYING GAMES IS MORE IMPORTANT THAN STUFF LIKE THIS.

!

I'LL GO UP AGAINST A WHOLE BUNCH OF DIFFERENT PLAYERS, RIGHT? LIKE YOU, AND SAEKI, AND...AND EVEN TOYA MEIJIN, RIGHT? RIGHT?

HOW SHOULD I KNOW?!

WAYA, DO YOU KNOW WHEN I'LL BE ABLE TO PLAY TOYA MEIJIN?

Yes, what if he keeps winning?

WHAT IF I KEEP WINNING? HOW ABOUT THEN, HUH?

Is that correct? Will you have an opportunity to play a match against that man?

IT TAKES ABOUT FIVE YEARS BEFORE SOMEONE AT YOUR LEVEL GETS TO FACE THE TOP PLAYERS.

IF YOU'RE RANKED BELOW 4-DAN, IT'LL TAKE ALL YOU'VE GOT JUST TO MAKE IT TO A SECOND-ROUND PRELIM MATCH!

IF YOU KEEP WINNING, SURE... YOU'LL GET TO THE TOP QUICKER. BUT YOU'VE GOT TO BE REALISTIC.

ME!

WE'RE IN THE SAME WORLD NOW, SO EVENTUALLY I'LL GET TO PLAY THEM ALL.

Yes, indeed!

BUT I'LL STILL BE IN THERE! I CAN PLAY TOYA AND EVEN HIS FATHER!

C'MON, GET REAL!

AND I WANNA PLAY OGATA 9-DAN AND THAT OLD HON'INBO GUY TOO!

I WANNA PLAY AGAINST MURAKAMI 2-DAN! I WENT UP AGAINST HIM IN THE YOUNG LIONS TOURNAMENT.

AKIRA TOYA!

BUT MOST OF ALL, I WANNA PLAY TOYA—

What about...

Hikaru...

...me?

Hikaru?

THE DRAW?

BUT YOUR OPPONENTS ARE SELECTED BY THE LUCK OF THE DRAW.

AKIRA'S STILL A LOWER-RANKED PLAYER, SO YOU COULD PLAY HIM... IF YOU GET LUCKY.

BUT I'M STILL IN THERE! I'LL BE ABLE TO PLAY THEM **EVENTUALLY**!

I TOLD YOU, YOU'RE **YEARS** AWAY FROM THE TOP PLAYERS!

OH! AND I'LL BE ABLE TO PLAY FOR REAL AGAINST SHIRAKAWA SENSEI AND MORISHITA SENSEI TOO!

You.
Not I...

That is correct, Hikaru. You are now a part of this world of go players.

Will you no longer allow me to play...?

Hikaru...

ASAHIKAWA
PALACE HOTEL **WELCOME**

48TH OZA TITLE MATCH

PALACE HOTEL

TEN MINUTES LEFT TILL GAME TIME...

VWSH

DING

18

GOOD
MORNING,
ZAMA
SENSEI.

GOOD
MORNING.

SNAP

THANK YOU.

OH, BY THE WAY... I DIDN'T GET A CHANCE TO CONGRATULATE YOU FOR DEFENDING THE MEIJIN TITLE FOR THE SIXTH TIME...

CONGRATULATIONS, TOYA SENSEI.

MAYBE YOU'RE RIGHT. PERHAPS FATIGUE DID GET THE BETTER OF ME DURING THE KISEI TOURNAMENT...

BUT YOU LET THE KISEI TITLE MATCH SLIP FROM YOUR GRASP... SEEMS TO ME YOU SCHEDULE TOO MANY GAMES AT ONCE. YOU'RE STRETCHING YOURSELF TOO THIN.

IT'S YOUR SON WHO'S AT THE TOP OF HIS GAME. I UNDERSTAND HE'S STILL UNDEFEATED.

SNAP

HMPH!

VURRR

HOWEVER, I'M READY TO TAKE YOU ON TODAY—WELL RESTED IN BOTH MIND AND BODY!

THE LAST GAME HE LOST WAS JUST BEFORE HE OFFICIALLY STARTED AS A PRO... IN THE SHINSHODAN SERIES.

THAT GAME HE LOST TO **YOU**, ZAMA SENSEI.

WELL, WELL...

HE'S WON 20 STRAIGHT GAMES.

SO TODAY YOU'RE OUT TO AVENGE YOUR SON, IS THAT IT?! HA HA HA!

VWSH

.....

HA HA...

AFTER YOU...

ZAMA SENSEI...

AUTHORIZED PERSONNEL ONLY

GOOD MORNING!

THE FIRST GAME FOR THE OZA TITLE

A-HA!

JAPAN GO ASSOCIATION

AN INTERESTING ARTICLE?

WHAT IS IT, KUWABARA SENSEI?

THE PRO TEST?

I WAS JUST LOOKING AT THE RESULTS OF THE PRO TEST.

SHINDO? WHO'S THAT?

HIS NAME'S SHINDO.

THAT LITTLE BRAT MADE IT.

谷康介(13)

進藤ヒカル(14)

和谷

I...SEE...

I PASSED HIM IN THE HALL ONE DAY.

ABOUT HALF A YEAR AGO.

ACTUALLY, IT WAS RIGHT AT THIS SPOT.

I GOT OUT OF THE ELEVATOR AND A GROUP OF INSEI YOUNGSTERS WERE HANGING AROUND.

IT'S KUWABARA SENSEI!

ACK! ~VWSH

HUH?

HM?

HE MAY BE PART OF THAT NEW WAVE OGATA WAS TALKING ABOUT...

I SENSED SOMETHING EXTRAORDINARY IN HIM...

EXTRAORDI-NARY? WELL, I LOOK FORWARD TO SEEING HIM PLAY THEN.

FWP

YES, INDEED.

I CAN'T WAIT, SAI!

SAI...?

THAT'S WHEN EVERYTHING STARTS.

SPRING...

YOU KNOW, SAI...

I WONDER WHO I'LL GET TO PLAY FIRST.

C'MON, LET'S PLAY!

WHAT'S WRONG?

And like him, they await his arrival.

Hikaru can't wait to play against the pros out there.

They await Hikaru's game, not mine...

KLAK

HAIKU CONTEST WINNERS!

12,794 SUBMISSIONS RECEIVED!

FIVE RUNNER-UPS!

THE GRAND PRIZE WINNER!

TAIKYOKU-
CHUU
JISHIN GA
OKITAYO
SHINDO GO

DURING A GO
GAME

AN EARTHQUAKE
SHOOK AND
RATTLED

SEISMIC SCALE
OF FIVE

(MANNAMI
SUZUKI)

Comment: Japan
Meteorological
Agency seismic
intensity scale

KINOKO KAKI
MEGANE TO
SEN KAKI
OCHI KANSEI

FIRST DRAW A
MUSHROOM

THEN DRAW
GLASSES AND
SOME LINES

THERE YOU HAVE
OCHI

(TADAYUKI
HONMA)

Comment: Now I
know how to draw
Ochi! (Obata)

THERE
WERE SO
MANY GREAT
ENTRIES
IT WAS
DIFFICULT
TO PICK OUT
WINNERS.
THANK YOU
ALL FOR
SENDING IN
YOUR HAIKU!

SENNEN NO
INISHIE NO
WAZA
IMA NI SAE

A THOUSAND-
YEAR-OLD

TALENT FROM THE
ANCIENT PAST

HERE IN THE PRESENT

(YUMI TOYODA)

Comment: Amazing!
Makes Sai sound
really cool! (Hotta)

ONNA DATO
OMOTTEITA
NONI
AH, SHOKKU

THOUGHT HE
WAS A GIRL

BUT I FOUND OUT
THAT HE'S NOT

AH, WHAT A BIG
SHOCK!

(ATSUSHI MIYUKI)

Comment: Does
it matter what
gender he is?
>laugh< (Obata)

NIHONMA NI
UTSU OTO
RIN TO
TOUYA-KE NO
ASA

JAPANESE-STYLE
ROOM

SOUNDS OF GO
STONES BOLDLY
PLAYED

TOYA'S HOUSE,
MORNING

(RYOTA SATO)

Comment:
Do they have rice
and natto for
breakfast?
(Hotta)

HIMITSU DAYO
TANSU NI
IPPAI
SHIROI
SUUTSU

IT'S A BIG
SECRET

THERE HIDDEN IN
HIS CLOSET

A BUNCH OF
WHITE SUITS

(KARUKARODON)

Comment:
I'd like to see
him in traditional
Japanese clothes.
(Hotta)

---

* Due to the ambiguity in how to pronounce the characters for entrants' names, some last names have been freely interpreted – Ed. note.

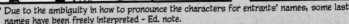

Game 98: "The Shinshodan Series"

AGH!

SKRTCH SKRNCH

WHADDAYA MEAN YOU CAME TO TELL US YOU MADE IT TO THE PROS?! WE ALREADY KNOW **THAT**!

SKRTCH

SKRNCH

WHY DIDN'T YA COME SOONER?! AFTER ALL, YOU OWE IT ALL TO **ME**!

WHY DO I OWE IT ALL TO YOU, MR. KAWAI?!

T-SHIRT DESIGNED BY TAKESHI OBATA

THE ONE THAT HIKARU WEARS!

THIS T-SHIRT WAS SOLD AT JUMP FESTA 2001

FRONT

BACK

Designed by Takeshi Obata

HE CAME TO PLAY HERE ALMOST EVERY DAY DURING HIS SUMMER BREAK.

YOU NEVER MET SHINDO, HUH?

THAT KID PASSED THE PRO EXAM?

YOU SAYING YOU **DON'T** OWE ME?!

YOU DON'T GET TO TAKE **ALL** THE CREDIT, MR. KAWAI!

THE RESULTS OF THE PRO TEST WERE ANNOUNCED IN *GO WEEKLY* A FEW ISSUES BACK. AH, HERE IT IS...

HMM... SHINDO HIKARU?

SEE?

YOU'RE CRAZY!

WHEN YOU WIN YOUR FIRST TITLE MATCH, HERE'S WHAT YOU SAY—"EVERYTHING I AM TODAY, I OWE TO MR. KAWAI!"

TOYA MEIJIN'S GOING TO WIN ANOTHER TITLE?

IT'LL BE **FIVE** FOR HIM SOON.

TITLE MATCH, EH? WHY DON'T YOU BE LIKE TOYA MEIJIN AND SNAG FOUR TITLES.

IF HE KEEPS HIS LEAD IN THE OZA SERIES, HE WILL.

HOW MANY MORE GAMES DOES HE HAVE TO WIN TO GET THE OZA TITLE?

HE'S ALREADY WON THE FIRST TWO GAMES. IT'S LOOKING PRETTY GOOD FOR HIM!

36

THE TENGEN SERIES? IS THAT A TITLE TOO?

BUT AT THE SAME TIME, HE'S DEFENDING HIS TENGEN TITLE. TOYA MEIJIN'S A BUSY MAN!

IT'S A FIVE-GAME SERIES, SO THREE GAMES NABS HIM THE TITLE.

YOU, YOU...

DID THIS KID *REALLY* MAKE IT TO THE PROS?

GUESS THE BOY'S STILL GOT A LOT TO LEARN BEFORE HE BECOMES A TITLE HOLDER HIMSELF.

READ OVER THESE OLD ISSUES OF GO WEEKLY. THAT'LL TEACH YOU SOMETHING ABOUT THE WORLD OF GO.

HERE YOU GO...

THIS HAS NOTHING TO DO WITH YOU, MR. KAWAI!

DON'T YOU BE AN EMBARRASS-MENT TO ME!

37

FWAP FWAP

HEY, THERE'S AKIRA'S DAD!

IT'S THE FIRST GAME OF THE OZA SERIES! AND HERE'S THE GAME RECORD!

THE REST IS ON THE BACK.

AND THIS IS...

HE'S PLAYING AGAINST ZAMA OZA. HE MUST BE THE CURRENT TITLE HOLDER.

Hikaru, only **part** of the game is recorded here...

THE FIRST GAME OF THE TENGEN SERIES. TOYA MEIJIN IS THE TITLE HOLDER AND ICHIRYU KISEI IS CHALLENGING HIM FOR IT.

HMM...

HEY, AKIRA'S DAD IS ON **THIS** ONE TOO.

HERE...

Turn the page, Hikaru!

...

I GUESS HE MUST BE PRETTY GOOD AFTER ALL.

HMM... TOYA MEIJIN TAKES HOME SIX STRAIGHT WINS.

Hikaru! Don't toss it down on the page I'm looking at!

WHAT ELSE IS IN HERE?

THIS IS FROM AUGUST, AND THIS IS FROM MAY.

THE DATES SKIP AROUND WITH THE REST OF THESE.

SOR-RY!

THAT'S PRETTY FAR BACK.

THE ONE ON THE BOTTOM'S FROM JANUARY!

HEY...

Hikaru! Turn the page!

OH, IT'S THE SHINSHODAN SERIES.

IT'S AKIRA! AND ZAMA OZA'S STANDING NEXT TO HIM.

IT'S THAT GAME WE ALL WATCHED ON THE MONITOR!

HERE!

FLP

IT SNOWED THAT DAY.

I'M GETTING PSYCHED!

THE SHINSHODAN SERIES...I ALMOST FORGOT ABOUT IT.

THIS IS THE GAME WHERE MY CAREER IS GOING TO BEGIN...

Hikaru, let me see that one too!

.....

...THE NEW YEAR.

AT THE BEGINNING OF THE NEW YEAR...

THANK YOU FOR GRANTING AN INTERVIEW SO EARLY IN THE YEAR.

ISN'T THAT RIGHT, AKIRA?

WHAT WITH ACQUIRING YOUR FIFTH TITLE AND ALL, YOU'LL BOTH BE VERY BUSY THIS YEAR.

I'LL DO MY BEST.

IT'S TOO BAD YOUR WINNING STREAK STOPPED AT 26 GAMES AT THE END OF LAST YEAR.

BUT WE'RE EXPECTING GREAT THINGS FROM YOU THIS YEAR.

THANK YOU FOR YOUR TIME.

I SUPPOSE I BETTER LET YOU GO...

YES?

AMANO...

WILL YOU BE PARTICIPATING THIS YEAR, SIR?

YOU MEAN THE SHINSHODAN SERIES?

ABOUT THAT SERIES THAT SETS UP THE NEW ROOKIE PROS AGAINST THE TOP VETERANS...

WE DIDN'T THINK WE SHOULD EVEN ASK YOU ABOUT IT THIS YEAR.

YOU WERE TOO BUSY TO PARTICIPATE LAST YEAR OR THE YEAR BEFORE.

I HAVEN'T SEEN HIM IN TWO YEARS.

IF I MAY, I'D LIKE TO REQUEST A SPECIFIC COMPETITOR.

!

BUT NOW HE'S FINALLY COME TO US...

WHP

THAT BASICALLY SHUTS DOWN MY COUNTER-ATTACK.

I GET IT...

YOU'VE GOT THIS SCARY EXPRESSION ON YOUR FACE LATELY...

SAI...

I KNOW YOU CAN'T READ THEM IF THEY AREN'T SPREAD OUT LIKE THIS, BUT...

BY THE WAY, IF I DON'T CLEAN UP THESE NEWSPAPERS, MY MOM'S GONNA KILL ME.

I've already memorized that man's games—the ones recorded on those papers.

That's fine. You may gather them together.

.....

SHINDO RESIDENCE.

KLK

OH, THAT'S RIGHT. MOM'S OUT SHOPPING.

50

THE SHINSHODAN SERIES?

YEAH.

UH...

RIGHT. SO WHO WILL I BE PLAYING?

YEAH, I KNOW.

YES, I UNDER-STAND.

OKAY.

RIGHT.

TOYA MEIJIN ?!

YOU KNOW—IN THE SHIN-SHODAN SERIES.

I GET TO PLAY AGAINST TOYA MEIJIN!

DID YOU HEAR THAT, SAI?!

I WONDER IF AKIRA WILL WATCH.

HEY!

REMEMBER LAST YEAR? WE WATCHED TOYA PLAY ZAMA OZA.

Hikaru...

ALL RIGHT! I'M GONNA SHOW HIM HOW STRONG A PLAYER I'VE GOTTEN TO BE!

HE'LL BE THERE FOR SURE!

HUH?

Please allow me to play against him.

53

進化せよ!! 君は意識に 過去を持つ
《飯田さとこ》

千年の 石音はるか 星の宙
《市瀬壮一》

YES,
ZAMA
OZA

CHEWS
ON HIS
FAN
NER-
VOUSLY

HE'S
GOT A
STRONG
JAW

(MAKIHARA
ASAMI)

好きなのは やっぱり読書か 本秀英?
《唐鎌希》

碁レンジャー 奈瀬はピンクな 紅一点
《島田真実》

ISUMI,
WAYA,

NASE,
OCHI
AND
TOYA

ALL
HAVE
SUCH
STRANGE
NAMES

(MATSUMOTO
CHIKA)

ヒカルの碁 悪手を打てば ヒカルの誤
《大澤亮太》

ネコの霊 憑いても変わらぬ みたにゃんこ
《石川真央》

成せば成る 奈瀬なら成れる 女流棋士
《谷川真里奈》

「ふざけるな!」アキラめません 勝つまでは
《阿部千春》

記念写真 ヒカルの後ろに 佐為うっすらと
《石毛翔太》

CHECKED
MY
HISTORY

TRIED
REAL
HARD
TO
LOOK
HIM UP

NOTHING
TO BE
FOUND

(MIYATA
AKI)

佐為の目は 最後に白い 星見据え
（3-1-5-2-4-6）
《柳田稔》

ジョジョみたい? 朝から晩まで ゴゴゴゴ碁!!
《小林慶治》

神の一手を 打ち間違えて 神一重
《井上剛志》

人の良さ 勝負強さと 紙一重
《吉原夏子》

太古の精 碁盤の前に 神と化す
《杉田遼》

平安に 咲き匂ひたり 彼岸花
《三木啓太郎》

藤原 佐為はヒカルの 才の元
《難波翔一朗》

白と黒 星を操り 夢ヒカル
《仁保裕司》

盤上に 輝く一手 ビッグバン!!
《西田じゅん》

さいの顔 ジャニーズ行っても 大丈夫
《矢羽樹史》

MISTER
TSUBAKI

NAME
OF A
PRETTY
FLOWER

FACE
OF A
GORILLA

(KATAHIRA
ERI)

いやし系 その笑顔 そばにおきたい
《田村梨奈》

膨らむ芽 思えば懐かし かたき種
《清水未央》

Game 99
"I'll Play"

Allow me to play...

Please, Hikaru...

SAI...

I want to play.

DON'T...

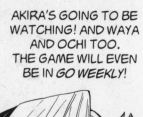

AKIRA'S GOING TO BE WATCHING! AND WAYA AND OCHI TOO. THE GAME WILL EVEN BE IN *GO WEEKLY!*

DON'T BE RIDICULOUS!

IF YOU PLAY, YOU'LL WIN FOR SURE. WE BOTH KNOW HOW STRONG YOU ARE.

AND BESIDES, IN THE SHINSHODAN SERIES, BLACK GETS A HANDICAP OF 5 1/2 POINTS IN REVERSE KOMI.

AND I'LL HAVE TO COVER UP FOR YOU AND ALL.

So what?

IT'S NOT THAT SIMPLE. I'M THE ONE WHO HAS TO DEAL WITH PUTTING ON AN ACT FOR YOU...

So... when will you ever let me play again?

SAI...

WHAT'S GOTTEN INTO YOU? I THOUGHT...

YOU TOLD ME YOU'VE GOT ALL OF ETERNITY ON YOUR SIDE, SO YOU'RE NOT IN ANY RUSH TO PLAY.

AFTER I DIE, YOU'LL BE BOUND TO SOMEBODY ELSE. YOU'LL HAVE PLENTY OF OTHER CHANCES TO PLAY. ISN'T THAT WHAT YOU TOLD ME?

OF COURSE IT IS! I WAS ONLY THE SECOND PERSON YOU ATTACHED YOURSELF TO. SO THERE'LL BE A THIRD AND A FOURTH.

Well, that's probably true, but...

......

WELL, ISN'T IT?

......

IS THAT WHAT THIS IS ALL ABOUT?

You don't know that for sure, Hikaru! I'm starting to worry about how much longer I'll be able to stay in this world...

HAVE THE **NEXT GUY** LET YOU PLAY ALL THE GAMES YOU WANT.

WELL, ANYWAY, THINGS GET TOO COMPLICATED WHEN YOU PLAY... SO JUST FORGET ABOUT IT.

Does this mean you will never allow me to play again?!

Hikaru!

Hikaru?

SCHEDULE

GENERAL ADMISSION PLAYING HALL 2ND FLOOR

INTERMEDIATE CLASS   2ND FLOOR

SHINSHODAN SERIES   5TH FLOOR

SCHEDULED MATCHES 5TH AND 6TH FLOORS

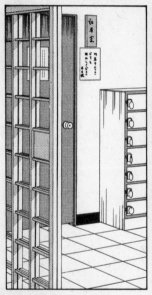

KCHK

IF IT ISN'T YOUNG OGATA.

IT'S BEEN A WHILE.

WELL, WELL...

AH...

KUWABARA SENSEI...

CHAK

YES... I LEARNED A LOT FROM THAT GAME.

WHEN WAS THE LAST TIME I SAW YOU FACE-TO-FACE LIKE THIS? THE HON'INBO MATCH? THAT SEVENTH GAME SURE WAS FUN! *HEH HEH HEH!*

64

AND I HEARD **YOU'RE** IN A BIT OF A SLUMP.

HEARD YOU TAUGHT KURATA A THING OR TWO THE OTHER DAY.

YOU'VE BEEN DOING QUITE WELL LATELY.

PUFF PUFF

BUT THE HON'INBO TITLE I'LL HOLD ON TO. WON'T GIVE THAT UP TO ANYONE.

IT'S MY AGE. I'VE LOST THE HUNGER.

MUCH BETTER THAN THAT TASTELESS CANDY CIGARETTE YOU HAVE THERE.

TRY ONE OF THESE, OGATA.

SO WHAT BRINGS THE ILLUSTRIOUS KUWABARA HON'INBO HERE TODAY?

WELL, I COULD ASK THE SAME OF YOU.

SO WHAT **DOES** BRING YOU HERE?

NO, THANK YOU.

HYAH HYAH!

SO WHAT IF TOYA MEIJIN'S PLAYING? THERE'S REALLY NO NEED FOR SOMEONE OF YOUR CALIBER TO COME WATCH THE GAME, OGATA.

TODAY'S JUST A MATCH IN THE SHINSHODAN SERIES.

SO YOU KNOW ABOUT SHINDO. HAVE YOU SEEN HIM PLAY BEFORE?

WHICH MUST MEAN THAT YOU SUSPECT THAT LITTLE BRAT IS ONE OF THE NEW WAVE OF PLAYERS TO WATCH OUT FOR. IS THAT IT?

SIXTH SENSE?

I JUST TOOK ONE LOOK AT THE KID AND I KNEW IT. HAH! MY SIXTH SENSE IS REALLY SOMETHING ELSE! HEH HEH.

AHA! SO I'M RIGHT ON TARGET!

HE JUST PASSED BY ME IN THE HALL AND I KNEW.

YOU KNOW... E.S.P.? INTUITION?

WHAT ABOUT YOU, WAYA?

THEY HAVEN'T CONTACTED ME YET.

SHINDO'S PLAYING IN THE FIRST GAME, AND YOU'RE PLAYING NEXT WEEK, OCHI. YOU GUYS ARE SO LUCKY!

JUST PASSED YOU IN THE HALL?! THAT'S RIDICULOUS!

I CAN'T WAIT TO PLAY TOO!

KCHK

BUT... WHY?!

LET'S SIT OVER HERE, OCHI.

OGATA 9-DAN AND KUWABARA HON'INBO?

HELLO, SIRS...

'CAUSE THEY'RE CURIOUS ABOUT SHINDO.

WHY WOULD TWO TOP PLAYERS LIKE THEM COME TO WATCH THE SHINSHODAN SERIES?

TOYA MEIJIN'S STUDY GROUP?

AND SHINDO ACTUALLY GOT INVITED TO ATTEND TOYA MEIJIN'S STUDY GROUP.

OGATA EVEN CAME TO WATCH SHINDO IN THE YOUNG LIONS TOURNAMENT.

.....

GUESS SHINDO MUST'VE CAUGHT HIS ATTENTION TOO.

BUT I DON'T KNOW WHAT THE DEAL IS WITH KUWABARA SENSEI...

HE WAS ALREADY PLANNING TO COME TO MY SENSEI'S STUDY GROUP.

BUT SHINDO SAID NO.

WHAT IS IT WITH SHINDO?

!

HE GOT TO BE A PRO WITH US... HE'S OUR RIVAL... AND HE'S OUR FRIEND!

KCHK

...AND KUWABARA SENSEI?

OGATA...

HELLO.

HI.

.....

YOU KNOW AKIRA TOYA?!

HELLO.

OCHI...

PLEASED TO MEET YOU. I'M AKIRA TOYA.

YES.

YOU'RE TOYA'S MEIJIN SON, AREN'T YOU?

70

HUH?

ERR, I... UH...

ARE YOU CURIOUS ABOUT SHINDO TOO?

DOESN'T THAT BEAT ALL?!

I SEE! THAT MEANS THE MEIJIN MUST BE TOO! HAH! THAT LITTLE BRAT'S EVEN GOT THE ATTENTION OF THE MEIJIN WITH HIS FIVE TITLES AND EVERYTHING!

KUWABARA SENSEI...

WHAT DO YOU SAY, OGATA...

THIS OUGHTA BE QUITE A MATCH.

CARE TO PUT A SMALL WAGER ON THE GAME?

AKIRA'S HERE TO WATCH THE GAME TODAY.

BA-BUMP

I KNOW AKIRA IS QUITE INTRIGUED BY YOU AND YOUR GAME.

I ACTUALLY REQUESTED THAT YOU BE MY OPPONENT IN TODAY'S MATCH.

BUT HE'S NOT ALONE. BOTH OGATA AND I ARE CURIOUS ABOUT YOU.

SHOW ME HOW STRONG YOUR GAME IS.

!

YES, I WILL!

NOW I'LL ACTUALLY BE PLAYING A MATCH HERE.

I TOOK A PEEK AT THIS ROOM LAST YEAR WITH WAYA.

BA-BUMP

BA-BUMP

YUGEN NO MA...

BA-BUMP

73

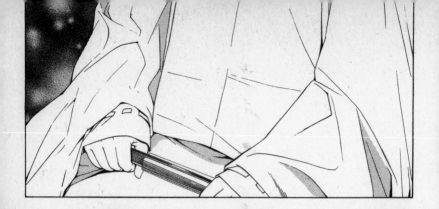

SAI!

Game 100 "Hikaru Takes His Time"

SAI...

SHINDO...?

MOVE, SAI!

SAI...

YOUNG MAN...

HAVE A SEAT.

SHINDO...

WHAT'S WRONG?

QUITE TEMPTING...

A WAGER, YOU SAY?

THE KID'S GOT A 5 1/2 POINT REVERSE KOMI HANDICAP... BUT HE'S UP AGAINST TOYA KOYO, THE MEIJIN TITLE HOLDER. IT'LL BE A TOUGH GAME FOR HIM.

YES...

A WAGER?!

I HIGHLY DOUBT THAT WILL BE THE CASE.

RIGHT. HE'S NOT THE TYPE.

UNLESS, OF COURSE, THE MEIJIN JUST CONSIDERS THIS MATCH AN EXERCISE AND LETS THE KID WIN.

HAH! I DON'T PLACE A BET UNLESS THERE'S A CHANCE OF A PAYOFF.

GOING FOR THE LONG SHOT?

SO. WHO ARE YOU BETTING ON?

THE BRAT.

OR ARE YOU SAYING **YOU** WANT TO PUT YOUR MONEY ON THE BRAT?

I HAVE NO DOUBT THAT HE WILL WIN.

I STUDY UNDER THE MEIJIN...

.....

HYAH HAH!

CLAP

CLAP

SHINDO...

HE GOT TO BE A PRO WITH US... HE'S OUR RIVAL... **AND HE'S** OUR FRIEND!

WHAT **IS** IT WITH SHINDO?

HE'S PLAYING A MATCH AGAINST MY FATHER, AND OGATA AND KUWABARA SENSEI HAVE BOTH TAKEN AN INTEREST IN THE GAME.

AND I'VE BEEN WAITING A LONG TIME...

HOW WILL HE PLAY?

HE'S COME A LONG WAY.

SHOW ME HOW STRONG YOUR GAME IS, SHINDO!

I just wanted to sit there for a little while.

I'm sorry, Hikaru.

SAI?

SHINDO!

I'VE GOT TO FOCUS ON THIS GAME.

DARN IT, SAI. DON'T GET ALL SULKY ON ME NOW.

BUT WHAT CAN I-?

I UNDERSTAND HOW YOU FEEL, BUT...

I MEAN, AFTER ALL...

SURE, A CHANCE LIKE THIS PROBABLY WON'T EVER COME UP AGAIN, BUT...

88

YOU'LL WIN FOR SURE, AND THEN PEOPLE WILL EXPECT ME TO LIVE UP TO THAT!

NO WAY! A 5 1/2 POINT REVERSE KOMI IS TOO MUCH OF AN ADVANTAGE FOR YOU.

IF YOU TAKE A HANDICAP, IT'LL CHANGE HOW YOU PLAY...

A HANDICAP...

BUT MAYBE...

SAY, SOMETHING LIKE 15 POINTS, THEN YOU WOULDN'T BE ABLE TO PLAY YOUR REGULAR GAME. WE MIGHT BE ABLE TO GET AWAY WITH IT...

IF WE GAVE YOU AN EVEN **BIGGER** HANDICAP...

IN THIS GAME, TOYA MEIJIN IS WHITE, AND HE'S TAKING A 5 1/2 POINT HANDICAP.

Yes! Let's do that!

SAI...

I'll play as if I have a 15-point handicap!

YOU REALLY WANT TO PLAY...? EVEN IN A MATCH LIKE THAT?

AND DON'T FORGET WHO YOUR OPPONENT IS. HE'LL **DESTROY** YOU.

DO YOU REALIZE WHAT YOU'RE SAYING, SAI? YOU HAVE THE FIRST MOVE, BUT OVERCOMING A 15-POINT HANDICAP WILL REALLY CHANGE YOUR GAME.

THE NEW PRO WILL TAKE BLACK WITH A REVERSE KOMI OF 5 1/2 POINTS. EACH PLAYER WILL HAVE TWO HOURS OF GAME TIME.

TIME TO BEGIN!

90

AFTER A PLAYER USES UP HIS GAME TIME, HE WILL HAVE ONE MINUTE TO COMPLETE EACH MOVE IN OVERTIME.

SAI...

PLEASE BEGIN.

ONEGAISHIMASU.

.....

ONEGAISHIMASU.

IF YOU'RE SURE YOU'RE ALL RIGHT WITH THAT HANDICAP...

OKAY...

HOW ARE YOU GOING TO PLAY THIS GAME...?

SAI...

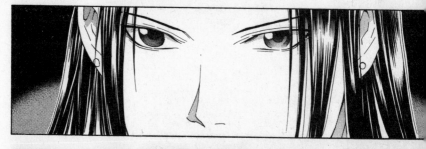

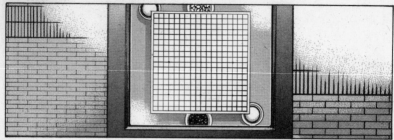

IT'S STARTED, RIGHT?

IT'S BEEN 20 MINUTES ALREADY...

"INTENSE"?

THE BRAT SURE IS INTENSE.

OR IS HE JUST TOO NERVOUS TO PICK UP A STONE?!

HYAH HA HA!

HE SHOULD HAVE DECIDED ON HIS FIRST MOVE LONG BEFORE THE GAME STARTED.

HE KNEW WHO HIS OPPONENT WOULD BE!

WHAT IS HE **THINKING**?

IT'S FOOLISH TO WASTE 20 MINUTES LIKE THIS!

EACH PLAYER HAS ONLY TWO HOURS.

YEAH, FOOLISH!

FOOLISH!

HE MUST BE UP TO SOMETHING.

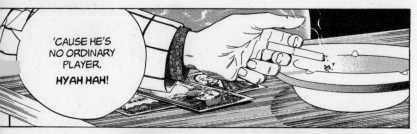

'CAUSE HE'S NO ORDINARY PLAYER.

HYAH HAH!

SHINDO...

SHINDO...

.....

I know how futile that is...

I must beat him by over 15 points.

Under normal circumstances, a game against an opponent such as this would surely be decided by half a point.

My opponent is no random player at a go salon.

His presence before the board is as it was before...

Regardless of the circumstances, in the end you will answer my moves.

.....

I must overwhelm my opponent or be completely overwhelmed myself.

I must win by over 15 points.

How far can I go?

Upper right star point!

.....

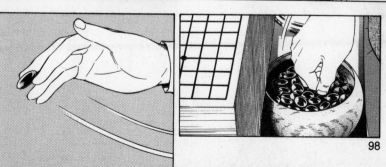

98

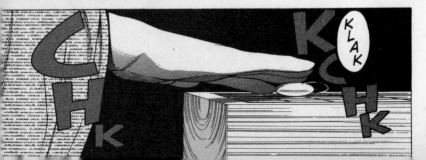

HIKARU **5** SHINDO

Game 101 "A Game Most Transparent"

Upper right star point!

CHK

KLAK

KLAK

I DON'T THINK ANYTHING LIKE THAT HAS EVER HAPPENED BEFORE.

THAT WORE ME OUT.

PHEW...

AKIRA TOYA HAS ARRIVED. LET'S GET **HIS** TAKE ON THIS.

AND IT DIDN'T LOOK LIKE SHINDO WAS PARTICULARLY NERVOUS.

LOUNGE

GAME IN PROGRESS
PLEASE KEEP DOORS CLOSED.

!

CHKK

OGATA SENSEI!

KUWABARA SENSEI IS HERE TOO?!

SHINDO CERTAINLY SURPRISED US—TAKING UP AN ENTIRE 20 MINUTES...

...JUST FOR HIS **OPENING** MOVE.

S**HUT**

SURE ATE UP A LOT OF TIME, EH, AMANO? IT'S NOT AS IF THE START OF THE GAME WAS DELAYED...

...RIGHT?

UH... THAT'S RIGHT, SIR.

I KNEW THE KID WAS SOMEBODY SPECIAL WHEN HE WALKED BY ME THE OTHER DAY.

THAT'S RIGHT.

KUWABARA SENSEI, ARE YOU HERE TO WATCH SHINDO PLAY?

OGATA... KEEP UNDERESTIMATING MY INTUITION AND YOU'LL NEVER BEAT ME!

"INTU-ITION"...?

YOU COULD TELL WITHOUT SEEING HIM PLAY?

WHAT?!

INTUITION— YOU KNOW, THAT SIXTH SENSE.

THAT'S RIGHT...

AND THEN THERE'S TOYA MEIJIN... HE **SPECIFICALLY REQUESTED** SHINDO FOR HIS OPPONENT IN THIS SERIES.

SHINDO SEEMS TO HAVE PIQUED **YOUR** INTEREST TOO, OGATA SENSEI.

WHATEVER IT WAS, SHINDO MUST HAVE DONE **SOMETHING** TO CATCH YOUR ATTENTION.

REQUESTED SHINDO?!

HE REQUESTED THE BRAT, EH?

AKIRA'S **RIVAL**?

ENOUGH ALREADY!

WAYA, WHAT'S—

MUST BE BECAUSE AKIRA CONSIDERS SHINDO A RIVAL OF SORTS...

WELL, THAT'S...

HE'S LIKE ME—GOT A HEALTHY SIXTH SENSE WORKING FOR HIM.

AKIRA'S GOT NOTHING TO DO WITH IT. TOYA MEIJIN IS INTRIGUED BY THE KID.

LOOK AT THAT!

WHY IS THERE MONEY ON THE TABLE?

SHINDO'S ATTACKING! WHY WOULD HE DO THAT THIS EARLY--?!

Cap the white stone.

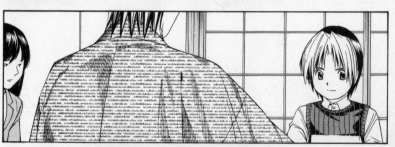

I won't have a chance unless I play aggressively right from the outset.

Now crawl.

I must draw my opponent into a complex battle to turn this into a contest of reading the game.

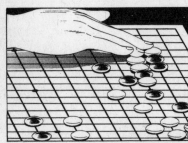

I shall intentionally leave openings that will tempt him to attack.

That's when Black will find a way out!

And when he puts everything on the line...

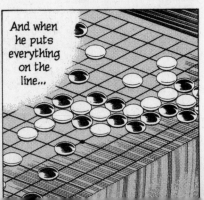

He's being exceedingly cautious.

However... he's not playing as I hoped.

Blocking move.

I must venture all.

From this point forward...

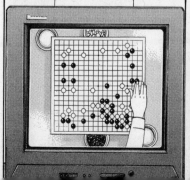

HE'S JUST PLAYING RECKLESSLY.

THIS IS BEYOND AGGRESSIVE...

WHAT IS SHINDO DOING?

TOYA, SHINDO IS *FAR* FROM BEING YOUR RIVAL.

THAT'S A BAD SHAPE.

HE'S OVER-PLAYING.

AFTER THIS STONE GETS TAKEN, IT'S ALL OVER FOR BLACK, RIGHT?

......

HMM...

THAT'S QUITE A TEMPTING MOVE.

FATHER WON'T DO IT.

WHAT DO YOU THINK, OGATA?

THE MEIJIN PROBABLY THOUGHT IT WOULDN'T BE APPROPRIATE TO END THE GAME SO EASILY.

HAH! IT'S HIS INTUITION.

BLACK CERTAINLY IS IN A BAD SPOT... BUT I CAN'T TELL WHAT TOYA MEIJIN IS THINKING.

* "Infinite Depth" - Scroll by Yasunari Kawabata.

THIS COULD END UP BEING RATHER TRICKY.

BUT IF I READ FURTHER AHEAD...

IT LOOKS AS IF BLACK WILL CRUMBLE HERE.

I BETTER NOT RESPOND TO MY OPPONENT'S INVITATION.

HIS GAME **APPEARS** TO BE ROUGH AND RECKLESS...

BUT CAREFUL CONSIDERATION IS GOING INTO EACH MOVE.

YET HE HAS...

THIS CHILD ONLY JUST TURNED PRO. HE'S 14 YEARS OLD.

AND THAT'S NOT ALL...

HOW...?

...SUCH COMPO- SURE.

...SUCH INTENSITY.

HE'S IN AN EXTREMELY DIFFICULT SPOT.

IT LOOKS LIKE SHINDO WENT UP AGAINST WHITE ALL OVER THE BOARD IN ORDER TO COMPLICATE THE SITUATION.

THE EXCHANGE THAT STARTED IN ONE SECTION HAS SPREAD THROUGHOUT THE ENTIRE BOARD.

THE TENDENCY TOWARD RECKLESSNESS IS THE PREROGATIVE OF YOUTH...

BUT THIS IS RIDICULOUS... AND AGAINST TOYA MEIJIN, NO LESS!

WE ALL KNOW WHAT'S GOING TO HAPPEN. BLACK IS COMPLETELY OVERWHELMED.

SHINDO...

THERE—HE
RESIGNED!

IT COMES TO AN END WITH NO SURPRISES. SHINDO WILL PROBABLY TAKE THIS PRETTY HARD.

SHUT

SKT

WELL...THE ANALYSIS WILL START SOON.

KLP

WAYA...

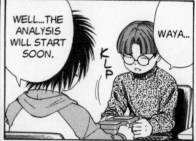

SKOOT

SKOOT

118

NOT AT ALL. THIS WAS QUITE AN INTRIGUING GAME.

SO ACCLAIM FOR SHINDO MUST BE POSTPONED.

IF THEY WERE TO PLAY AGAIN, I'D **STILL** PUT MY MONEY ON THE KID.

YOU KNOW...

JUST A SEC'...

AKIRA...

KUWABARA SENSEI...

SHUT

...IF SHINDO **DELIBERATELY** GAVE HIMSELF A HUGE HANDICAP, THE WAY HE PLAYED THE GAME MAKES PERFECT SENSE.

WONDERING ABOUT THIS MATCH, EH?

WELL, IT SEEMS TO ME THAT...

SHINDO GAVE HIMSELF A HANDICAP?

?

HYAH HA HA HA!

BUT... THAT'S CRAZY!

AGAINST **MY** FATHER?!

BUT HE CERTAINLY IS AN INTERESTING FELLOW.

WHY HE WOULD DO SUCH A THING IS BEYOND ME!

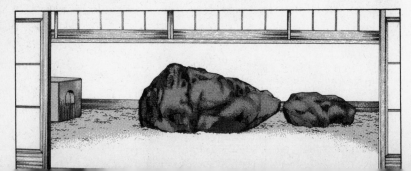

That's
it
then...

.....

I WOULD'VE
PREFERRED A
GAME WITHOUT
A HANDICAP.

BUT YOU CANNOT HIDE WHAT LIES BENEATH IT.

I CAN'T FATHOM WHY YOU WOULD PLAY LIKE THIS...

GASP!

I'M LOOKING FORWARD TO OUR NEXT GAME.

...BUT HE ALSO SENSED SAI'S **TRUE STRENGTH.**

THROUGHOUT THE GAME, I FELT IN YOU AN INTENSITY CHARACTERISTIC OF THE **MOST SEASONED** VETERANS.

NEXT TIME, WE'LL PLAY AN EVEN MATCH...

Yes...
Someday...

.....

WELL THEN, LET'S START FROM THE BEGINNING ...

THANK YOU, EVERYBODY.

127

HE GAVE HIMSELF A HANDICAP?!

HYAH HAH HA!

BUT WHY?!

THAT SHINDO CERTAINLY IS AN INTERESTING FELLOW, EH?

WELL!

I PLAYED HIM TWO YEARS AGO...

AND HE WAS **SO STRONG** THAT I FELT LIKE I WAS PLAYING AGAINST MY FATHER.

CHK

.....

I JUST DON'T GET HIM.

BUT THEN, HALF A YEAR LATER, I PLAYED HIM AGAIN, AND HIS GAME WAS **SO WEAK** IT WAS LIKE PLAYING A COMPLETELY DIFFERENT PERSON.

I DIDN'T HAVE ANY INTENTION OF CONSIDERING SOMEONE SO WEAK AS A RIVAL...

HOW ODD.

A DIFFERENT PERSON...

...HE TOLD ME...

BUT THEN...

SOMEDAY, THE REAL ME IS GOING TO CATCH UP TO YOU!

IF YOU KEEP CHASING AFTER SOME ILLUSION OF ME...

...AFTER PLAYING MY FATHER IN THE SPECIAL YUGEN NO MA ROOM!

AND HERE HE IS NOW...

PRIVATE:
GO COMPETITORS ONLY

THE NEXT TIME I SAW HIM, HE'D BECOME AN INSEI.

I GUESS THAT MEANS **YOU** LED HIM TO THE WORLD OF THE PROS, HUH?

GAME IN PROGRESS
PLEASE KEEP DOORS CLOSED.

TOYA... UH... WHAT'S YOUR FIRST NAME AGAIN?

I'LL HAVE TO REMEMBER THAT.

AKIRA TOYA. YES...

AKIRA...

IVATE:
GO
ETITORS
ONLY

GAME

TOYA...

WHAT'S HAPPENING IN THERE?

.....

HE JUST CLAMMED UP AND WON'T TALK TO ANYBODY.

WHAT'S UP WITH SHINDO?

...AN EVEN MATCH.

BUT STILL, TOYA'S FATHER IS REALLY **SOMETHING.** HE **KNEW** YOU WEREN'T JUST PLAYING RECKLESSLY...

I DON'T THINK HE COULD TELL EXACTLY HOW STRONG YOU REALLY ARE...

I WONDER IF THAT'S POSSIBLE...

OF COURSE, I KNOW WHAT YOU **REALLY** WANT IS TO PLAY AN EVEN MATCH AGAINST HIM, SAI.

"Some-day"?!

WELL, MAYBE SOMEDAY WE'LL BE ABLE TO DO SOMETHING ABOUT IT...

What?! You wonder...? What does that mean?

YOU KNOW I CAN'T GIVE YOU A DEFINITE DATE!

BUT YOU RUINED EVERYTHING BY BEING SO SELFISH!

THIS SHOULD'VE BEEN AN IMPORTANT GAME FOR **ME**, YOU KNOW!

UMM...

UH...

.....

I GUESS IT'S JUST YOUR **BAD LUCK** THAT YOU CAME INTO MY CONSCIOUS-NESS.

HMPH...

I'm sorry...

HE WAS TRYING TO BECOME A PRO TOO, RIGHT?

WHY DIDN'T HE PLAY HIS **OWN** GAMES?

YOU CALLED HIM "TORAJIRO,"* RIGHT?

I BET YOU WERE **A LOT HAPPIER** WITH SHUSAKU. **HE** LET YOU PLAY ALL YOU WANTED, DIDN'T HE?!

*The go master's childhood given name, from before he became the 14th generation Hon'inbo master

It was my fault!

The truth is, Hikaru...

HOLD ON...

When I found myself back in this world, I panicked. I didn't know I would ever have another chance. I pleaded with Torajiro to not let this opportunity pass me by. I was selfish...

What--?!

...DIED EARLY BECAUSE OF YOU?

COULD IT BE THAT TORAJIRO...

Torajiro was a kind and generous soul. There was an epidemic, and he helped the sick people around him. He was fully aware of the danger.

No! It's not like that at all!

And that's how he...

Torajiro was an intelligent and compassionate person.

So you see...

.....

WELL, EXCUSE ME FOR BEING SO MEAN AND DUMB!

Hikaru keeps improving, and I am unable to play.

What purpose do I serve inside Hikaru's consciousness?

FINE, THEN...

FWMP

HMPH!

HOW 'BOUT I TAKE YOU SOMEWHERE TO CHEER YOU UP?

HEY! THOSE PEOPLE ARE PLAYING GO ON COMPUTERS!

THERE'S SO MUCH STUFF GOING ON—LECTURES, TEACHING GAMES, AND...

So many people playing go!

CHATTER

CHATTER

CHATTER

Hikaru! Let's go watch a game!

SO MANY PEOPLE SHOWED UP, EVEN THOUGH IT'S WAY OUT HERE IN THE BOONIES!

AMATEUR DIFFERENTIAL
6 DAN MATCH
REGISTRATION

I FOUND OUT ABOUT THIS EVENT IN GO WEEKLY.

I GUESS I MESSED THINGS UP...

THERE'S NO WAY THAT GAME HE PLAYED WITH TOYA MEIJIN COULD HAVE BEEN SATISFYING...

IT TOOK A WHILE TO GET HERE, BUT IT WAS WORTH IT.

LOOKS LIKE THIS IS CHEERING SAI UP!

OCHI AND WAYA BOTH TORE MY GAME APART, SO I'M GOING TO GET REVENGE!

HEY, SAI! LET'S GO WATCH OCHI'S SHINSHODAN GAME NEXT WEEK, OKAY?

Never again shall I...

I am the one at fault.

He's right about my being selfish. I prevented him from playing a game that would have been important for his development.

Hikaru's trying to make me feel better...

But I swear I'll only ask him to let me play once in a while...

Oh, I can't promise that...

141

THANK YOU VERY MUCH—THAT'LL BE ¥1500.*

*about $13

I HAVEN'T SOLD **THAT** BOARD YET, BUT I DID SELL THREE **OTHERS.**

...GOKISO SENSEI!

STOP SELLING THOSE CHEAP *SENSU* FANS AND WORK ON MOVING THOSE PRICEY GO BOARDS OF YOURS...

THIS TYPE HERE—REAL *KAYA* WOOD FOR ¥200,000!*

WHICH ONES?

*about $1,700

GIMME THAT PEN.

NOT SO LOUD, SENSEI!!

REAL KAYA, EH? WELL, I SUPPOSE YOU COULD FOOL AN AMATEUR WITH THOSE. WHAT'S THAT RETAIL FOR NORMALLY—ABOUT ¥80,000?*

*about $690

NOW **THAT'LL** MOVE THEM!

YOU JUST WRITE "ON SALE"...

*about $2,600   **about $1,700

DON'T BE SILLY... I'M A PROFESSIONAL GO PLAYER.

AH-HA! SENSEI, YOU MIGHT HAVE MORE OF A TALENT FOR BUSINESS THAN ME!

DON'T WORRY! I'VE GOT IT COVERED.

DON'T FORGET—I'M THE ONLY REASON THEY LET YOU IN HERE. YOU BETTER WORK HARD AND MAKE IT WORTH MY WHILE!

Slow down, Sai!

I GUESS IT USED TO BE SERIALIZED IN *JUMP.*

JANUARY NEW ARRIVALS

CYBORG JIICHAN G 21st Century edition ①

CYBORG JIICHAN G?

ROOKIES

Kochira Katsushikaku ...mae

The dialogue's not quite there yet.

BOOORING...

THIS IS A MANGA ABOUT A BORING OLD MAN'S GAME!

Hikaru no Go ①

GRMP

WHAT'RE YOU TALKING ABOUT?!

I want Hotta Sensei's autograph!

HEY, *HIKARU NO GO* IS PRETTY GOOD!

HIKARU VS. G-CHAN

①

HIKARU NO GO 4-PANEL MANGA

Game 103 "Forgery"

EVERYONE AT THIS EVENT IS PRETTY WEAK.

C'mon, Hikaru!

OPEN GAMES

All those stones are in atari! His next move is obvious.

IT'S A NO-BRAINER!

HMM...

WHAT?!

KLAK

GUESS THOSE STONES ARE GONERS...

Argh! He missed it! He made a completely different move!

KLAK

COME ON—**SAVE** YOURSELF! CONNECT THAT GROUP!

Black missed too!

YOU CAN STILL SIGN UP.

WOULD YOU LIKE TO PLAY?

HA HA HA!

This is more intense than watching a professional match!

THEY'RE SELLING STUFF OVER THERE. LET'S GO TAKE A LOOK!

Oops! I just told myself I wouldn't...

Well, if you don't want to, I'll—

HUH? OH, NO THANKS!

THOSE BOWLS ARE MADE OF KAYA, AND THE PRICE IS...

What did you expect?

Snacks and manga?

OH... THEY'RE ONLY SELLING GO STUFF.

GO BOARDS, EH? HMM...

I'LL BE WAITING!

I'LL COME BACK.

HOW ABOUT **NOW**? WHY WAIT UNTIL **SOMEDAY**?

WELL, I'M NOT THAT GOOD...

I'D LIKE TO HAVE A NICE ONE SOMEDAY.

THIS ONE HERE IS ¥200,000 AND THAT ONE IS ¥250,000.

THEY SAY YOU IMPROVE MORE QUICKLY IF YOU STUDY ON A HIGH-QUALITY BOARD.

BOTH ARE MADE FROM THE **HIGHEST QUALITY KAYA**. AND YOU WON'T GET A BETTER DEAL THAN TODAY'S SALE PRICE.

That's not kaya. It looks similar, but it's definitely not kaya.

Kaya?! He calls that kaya?!

"KAYA"?

SAI, WHAT'S KAYA?

WHAT ABOUT MINE?

Yours is katsura wood.

All the best boards are made of kaya!

Kaya is a type of wood used for go boards. Torajiro's board was made out of kaya! Your grandfather's board is made out of kaya, too.

WHAT--?!

IT'S NOT REAL KAYA?

SO THAT'S A LIE?

GOKISO SENSEI!

QUIT INTERFERING WITH MY BUSINESS!

WHAT'S ALL THE FUSS ABOUT OVER HERE?

STOP TALKING NONSENSE, KID!

KCHK

A STONE?

Hikaru, place a stone on the board.

I WASN'T INTER-FERING...

HEY, WHAT'RE YOU--?!

HMPH!

KLAK

This isn't kaya—it's some other wood.

Now I'm **positive**! The sound is **duller** than it would be if it were kaya!

YOU LITTLE BRAT! STOP HANDLING THE MERCHANDISE!

ACK!

WHAT'S THIS ALL ABOUT?

WHAT'S GOING ON HERE?

HEY!

YEAH, BUT...

UH, NOT REALLY... THIS KID JUST DROPPED A STONE ON A BOARD I WAS TRYING TO SELL, THAT'S ALL.

IS THERE A PROBLEM?

I THINK I'LL WAIT UNTIL I CAN PLAY A LITTLE BETTER.

UH... I'LL PASS ON THE BOARD FOR NOW.

YOU PUT A MARK ON THAT BOARD! ARE YOU GONNA BUY IT NOW?

THAT'S ENOUGH OUTTA YOU!

HMPH!

SHUF SHUF RUSH

HEY, DON'T–

I'M SORRY...

SO DON'T DO THAT AGAIN!

GO BOARDS ARE MADE OF WOOD, AND WOOD CAN GET MARKED UP WHEN YOU PUT A STONE ON THE BOARD.

THE SUCKERS AREN'T BITING TODAY.

HUH?!

HON'INBO SHUSAKU'S PERSONAL BOARD? WOW!

Yes, but...

SAI, YOU TOLD ME TO DO IT!

Where? Where? Let me see!

THIS IS FOR SALE?! FOR ¥6,000,000?!*

*about $51,900

I ACQUIRED THAT JUST RECENTLY FROM AN ANTIQUE SHOP.

READ THIS WAY

IT WAS USED BY SHUSAKU SENSEI WHEN HE HAD A POST TEACHING GO IN TAKAMATSU.

HUH?!

TA-DUM

WERE YOU GUYS EVER IN TAKAMATSU?

We traveled throughout the land.

DURING THAT TIME, SHUSAKU SENSEI WAS ASKED TO SIGN THAT BOARD.

GOKISO SENSEI!

In Takamatsu?

Did he sign a board in Takamatsu...?

YES, AND THIS IS THAT VERY BOARD!

安政四丁巳晩夏書

本因坊秀策

AND IF YOU BUY **TODAY**, I'LL MAKE YOU AN INCREDIBLE OFFER—**ZERO PERCENT INTEREST.**

YOU COULD PAY IN INSTALLMENTS OF 50 OR 100.

BUT SIX MIL—THAT'S QUITE EXPENSIVE.

Hikaru! That's not Torajiro's handwriting!

SO THAT MEANS...

...IT'S A FAKE?!

YOU AGAIN! THIS IS 100 PERCENT GENUINE! IT'S THE REAL THING!

AH! WAIT, SIR!

WHY DON'T YOU JUST GO AWAY.

THAT'S NOT SHUSAKU'S WRITING!

How can he claim it's 100 percent genuine?!

OH, I GET IT! THAT'S **YOUR** WRITING, ISN'T IT?

A PRO? BUT WHY WOULD HE LIE LIKE THAT?

THERE'S NO MISTAKE. THIS IS THE REAL THING.

SEE?! AND THAT'S COMING FROM A **PRO** PLAYER.

WHAT?!

Ignominious wretch! That forgery sullies Torajiro's name!

HUH?! IGNO-RAMUS REX?

OKAY, OKAY!

HOW DARE YOU DISRESPECT GOKISO SENSEI LIKE THAT?!

GOKISO SENSEI, YOUR TEACHING GAMES ARE ABOUT TO BEGIN. IF YOU'D PLEASE...

.....

HEH! WHO'D BELIEVE A BRAT LIKE YOU, ANYWAY?

AND **YOU**... COME HERE.

THEY'RE NOT MADE OF **REAL KAYA**, EITHER!

IT'S A FAKE FOR SURE! THOSE TWO ARE LIARS! AND THOSE OTHER BOARDS...

IS IT TRUE? THAT'S A FORGERY? HOW CAN YOU TELL?

I THOUGHT SO!

!

THEY MUST BE **SHIN KAYA**.

I HAD A FEELING THOSE BOARDS WEREN'T REAL.

YOU KNEW?

OUR REGULAR VENDOR—THE ONE WHO CAME UNTIL THIS YEAR—WAS VERY NICE. HE TOOK THE TIME TO EXPLAIN EVERYTHING.

I'M NO EXPERT, BUT...

IT'S RESISTANT TO CRACKS AND MOLD, SO IT'S PERFECT FOR GO BOARDS.

SHIN KAYA HAS A BEAUTIFUL GRAIN VERY SIMILAR TO REAL KAYA, BUT IT'S ACTUALLY AN IMPORTED WOOD CALLED SPRUCE.

HE SOUNDS A LOT BETTER THAN THIS ONE!

WHY DIDN'T YOUR USUAL GUY COME BACK?

BUT BOARDS MADE FROM **REAL** KAYA ARE MUCH MORE EXPENSIVE, SO SOME UNDERHANDED MERCHANTS SELL SHIN KAYA BOARDS AS REAL KAYA.

WE COULDN'T REFUSE.

GOKISO SENSEI **INSISTED**...

WELL, I'LL GO DEAL WITH THAT VENDOR NOW. THANKS FOR YOUR HELP, AND ENJOY THE REST OF YOUR TIME HERE!

I'VE HEARD SOME BAD RUMORS ABOUT HIM... YES...

I GUESS WE COULD CHECK OUT SOME MORE GAMES.

THAT SURE PUT A DAMPER ON THINGS.

OH, BOY...

OR IS THERE SOMETHING ELSE YOU'D LIKE TO DO?

SAI...

I CAN'T SEE MYSELF DOING THAT.

THAT GUY OVER THERE BY THAT GIANT GO BOARD IS GIVING A LECTURE OR SOMETHING. IS HE A PRO? I WONDER IF I'LL HAVE TO DO STUFF LIKE THAT SOMEDAY.

UH-OH... YOU'RE REALLY STEAMED...

UH, SAI...?

Hikaru, over there...

HUH?

TEACHING GAMES

TEACHING GAMES

That man is over there now, playing teaching games.

OH...

AND HE'S PLAYING THE MAN WHO ALMOST BOUGHT THAT GO BOARD...

162

TEACHING GAMES

LOOK—YOU'VE GOT WEAK POINTS EVERYWHERE.

MAYBE YOU NEED TO STUDY ON A HIGH-QUALITY BOARD AFTER ALL, EH?

MY STONES IN THE UPPER RIGHT ARE DEAD NOW TOO...

That cruel man is tormenting a weak player.

I CAN'T BELIEVE THIS GAME!

.....

You can! It's not over yet!

What kind of teaching game is that?!

I CAN'T...

I THINK THAT'S IT...

HUH?

YOU CAN STILL DO IT, MISTER!

IT'S NOT OVER YET.

I DIDN'T SAY THAT!

FINE THEN, LET'S CONTINUE.

HMM? YOU THINK YOU STILL HAVE A CHANCE?

THE KID BEHIND YOU THINKS YOU CAN MAKE A COMEBACK FROM THIS.

HUH?!

HERE, BE MY GUEST!

S K O O T

WELL, COME ON THEN. LET'S SEE YOU BACK UP THAT BIG MOUTH OF YOURS.

CHFF CHFF

You might not be able to accomplish this, Hikaru, but I can!

ARE YOU SURE, SAI? THIS GUY MIGHT BE A JERK, BUT HE IS A PRO.

S K O O T

BUT IF YOU **CAN'T**... THEN YOU HIGHTAIL IT OUT OF HERE ON THE DOUBLE!

Sit down, Hikaru!

TH-THANKS FOR THE GAME.

OKAY.

Tell him that if I win, he has to remove that fake Tora-jiro board!

HEY!

!

FINE! BUT IF I BEAT **YOU**, THEN YOU HAVE TO GET RID OF THAT FAKE SHUSAKU BOARD.

WELL?

SKOOT

SWP

BUT, SAI... WHAT IF HE DRAWS A LOT OF ATTENTION TO US AFTER YOU BEAT HIM?

I'LL TAKE THAT AS A PROMISE.

HMPH! AS IF THAT WOULD EVER HAPPEN.

He'll be too embarrassed to talk about a loss against you.

He thinks you're an amateur, a mere child.

GO FOR IT, SAI!

THAT MEANS YOU DON'T HAVE TO PULL ANY PUNCHES...

One-point corner enclosure!

FINE! WE'LL SETTLE THIS WITH A GAME OF GO!

I HAVEN'T BEEN IN A 4-PANEL GAG MANGA IN TEN YEARS!

BUT...

HIKARU VS. G-CHAN

②

I CAN'T COME UP WITH ANYTHING FUNNY!

I CAN'T...

A GAP OF TEN YEARS!

KLAK

HOTTA SENSEI! HELP!

KLAK

HIKARU NO GO 4-PANEL MANGA

SHINDO
HIKARU

KURATA SENSEI, OUR TIME IS ALMOST UP.

ANY QUESTIONS UP TO THIS POINT?

WELL, THIS IS A GOOD STOPPING POINT. I GUESS THAT'S IT THEN.

THANKS ... THANK YOU.

I HOPE SO TOO!

I HOPE YOU GET A TITLE THIS YEAR!

THE MEIJIN TITLE WOULD SURE BE NICE!

SURE.

KURATA SENSEI, MAY I HAVE AN AUTOGRAPH?

THERE! "KURATA ATSUSHI, FUTURE MEIJIN"!

I'LL EVEN PUT IT IN WRITING!

NEXT—THE KISEI TITLE!

SENSEI, MAY I HAVE YOUR AUTOGRAPH TOO?

HA HA HA!

I'LL BE SURE NOT TO LET TOYA MEIJIN SEE THIS.

LET'S SEE... THINK I'LL GO WITH "CLIMBING UP KISEI"!

SWP

AND IT'S **TRUE**! YOU HAVE THE POTENTIAL TO ACQUIRE **ANY ONE** OF THOSE TITLES!

HOW ABOUT A HON'INBO ONE FOR ME?

YES, OF COURSE!

I'VE RESERVED A TEACHING GAME WITH YOU, SENSEI! YOROSHIKU ONEGAISHIMASU!

SWP

"HONING IN ON HON'INBO"!

INSTEAD OF GOKISO SENSEI...

I SHOULD HAVE RESERVED A GAME WITH KURATA SENSEI TOO...

THAT'S MEAN! WHY'S HE IN SUCH A FOUL MOOD?

I HAD A FIVE-STONE HANDICAP, BUT IT WAS LIKE HE JUST KEPT SETTING TRAPS FOR ME TO FALL INTO.

A "BEAT-ING"?

I JUST CAME FROM HIM, AND HE GAVE ME SUCH A BEATING...

WHY DO YOU SAY THAT?

BUT THAT'S NO EXCUSE TO PICK ON AMATEUR GO ENTHUSIASTS LIKE US!

I HEARD A RUMOR HE'S UPSET LATELY BECAUSE HE LOST BIG IN THE STOCK MARKET.

HA HA! COMING BACK FROM A LOSING POSITION AGAINST A PRO IS ALL BUT IMPOSSIBLE!

BUT SOME KID SAID HE COULD COME BACK FROM MY POSITION ON THE BOARD.

I RE-SIGNED AND LEFT AS SOON AS I COULD.

AREN'T YOU THE ONE WHO JUST LEFT GOKISO SENSEI'S TEACHING GAME?

IF THAT KID PULLS IT OFF, THEN HE'S STRONGER THAN MOST PROS.

NO WAY!

WELL, THAT KID FINISHED YOUR GAME—AND HE WON!

YES, THAT WAS ME.

IT'S TRUE. IT JUST SORT OF... WORKED OUT!

REALLY?

DASH

THIS GAME IS OVER.

THAT'S IT.

YOU MAKE MOVES I WOULDN'T DREAM OF.

YOU'RE AMAZING, SAI...

...AND IT WOULD HAVE BEEN IMPOSSIBLE FOR ME TO COME BACK FROM THAT GAME.

I KEPT THINKING ABOUT HOW I WOULD'VE PLAYED...

!

WHAT HAPPENED? LET'S SEE!

NO...

HOW... HOW COULD THIS HAVE...?

OTHER-WISE, THIS NEVER COULD HAVE...

IT'S BECAUSE I COM-PLETELY UNDERES-TIMATED HIM.

IS THIS THE GAME?

KASHUF

SHFF

KURATA...

QUITE AN EMBARRASSING GAME I PLAYED...

SHFF

SHFF

HEY! AW...

SKOOT

YOU'D LAUGH IF YOU SAW IT...

CHFF

177

HEY...

DON'T FORGET YOUR PROMISE!

SURE WISH I COULD'VE SEEN IT...

YOU KNOW...

SO YOU **WON**, RIGHT?

YOU MADE A COMEBACK FROM PRETTY FAR BEHIND.

I JUST HEARD SOMEONE TALKING ABOUT THIS GAME...

SHFF

SHFF

HEY...

BUT YOUR OPPONENT WAS A PRO. YOU MUST BE—

THAT **IS** WHAT HAPPENED, RIGHT?

SHFF

178

AMATEUR IGO FESTIVAL

SEEMS LIKE I'VE SEEN YOU BEFORE...

I'M SHINDO.

I'LL BE A PRO STARTING THIS YEAR.

ARE YOU A PRO?

SO WHAT DID GOKISO PROMISE YOU?

RIGHT! I READ ABOUT YOU IN *GO WEEKLY!* YOU PLAYED THAT SHINSHODAN GAME!

OH...

179

WELCOME, WELCOME...

KURATA SENSEI!

IT'S NOT EVEN WORTH YOUR TIME TO WINDOW SHOP!

SENSEI, NONE OF MY MERCHANDISE ON DISPLAY TODAY IS WORTHY OF YOUR DISCRIMINATING EYE!

GENUINE KAYA GO BOARD
ON ¥ ~~300000~~
SALE 200000

REAL KAYA... FOR ¥200,000?

WELL?

PARDON?! OH, WELL... YOU SEE... UH...

WHAT'S WITH THIS PRICE TAG?

UMM...

GOOD THING YOU NOTICED!

AH, SEE? HERE'S THE RIGHT PRICE!

A MISTAKE! OH MY!

*about $700

I'LL TRACK THEM DOWN AND EXPLAIN THE SITUATION.

IF THEY USED YOUR INSTALLMENT PLAN, YOU MUST HAVE THEIR CONTACT INFO.

HUH? NO, I—

YOU PROBABLY ALREADY SOLD SOME AT THAT PRICE...

AND THEN THERE'S **THIS** MATTER...

YOU'LL TRACK THEM DOWN?

SOUNDS GOOD.

I CAN'T REALLY TELL WHETHER THIS IS SHUSAKU'S HANDWRITING OR NOT.

HMM... WELL...

I'M SURE!

I'M SURE!

YOU'RE SURE?

It's fake!

IT'S FAKE!

SO THIS IS--?

I JUST **KNOW** IT IS!

YOU JUST "**KNOW**," HUH?

I'D LIKE YOU TO REMOVE "SHUSAKU'S" BOARD FROM YOUR DISPLAY.

THIS BOARD...

183

A PIECE OF ADVICE, THOUGH... DON'T BE TOO PROUD OF YOURSELF FOR BEATING GOKISO.

BECAUSE YOU JUST **KNOW** IT'S FAKE, EH? HA HA HA!

Do it—right now!

NOW IF YOU BEAT **ME**, THAT'S A DIFFERENT STORY.

UMM... SO WHO ARE YOU?

Who is this fellow?

THAT GUY'S IN A SLUMP—JUST ABOUT **EVERYONE** BEATS HIM.

ER... SO YOUR NAME'S KURATA...?

ARE YOU REALLY THAT STRONG A PLAYER?

I'M GOING TO TAKE THE MEIJIN TITLE SOME-DAY—OR MAYBE THE KISEI OR HON'INBO OR...

WHAT?! I'M A PRO TOO! I'M **KURATA**! YOU HAVEN'T HEARD OF ME?!

BUT I'M TELLING YOU... IT'S NOT SO DIFFICULT TO TAKE DOWN THE ONES AT THE TOP.

TIME WILL TELL...

HE'S DOING EVERYTHING HE CAN TO AVOID **LOSING** HIS TITLE. IT'S ONLY A MATTER OF TIME...

BUT THAT KUWABARA SENSEI—IT'S ALL AN ACT. HE'S PANICKING.

EVERYONE UP THERE IS STRUGGLING TO **MAINTAIN** THEIR POSITION. TOYA MEIJIN MIGHT BE AT HIS PEAK RIGHT NOW...

IF I DON'T GET IT, THEN MAYBE IT'LL BE OGATA... **ONE** OF US WILL GET THAT HON'INBO TITLE.

PERSONALLY, I'M MORE AFRAID OF THE PLAYERS WHO ARE **UNDER** ME.

IT'S LIKE A **DEATH MATCH** WHEN I PLAY SOMEONE RANKED **BELOW** ME.

I'M MORE AFRAID OF **AKIRA** TOYA THAN I AM OF **KOYO** TOYA.

Oh, my! He is confident!

HA HA! AND TAKE THEM DOWN, I WILL!

BUT FOR NOW, I STILL HAVE TO TAKE DOWN THOSE **AT THE TOP!**

HIKARU SHINDO.

WHAT DID YOU SAY YOUR NAME WAS?

HEY, HAND ME A WHITE SENSU FAN.

THERE AREN'T MANY PLAYERS AROUND WHO HAVEN'T HEARD OF ME.

AND A PEN TOO.

HM?

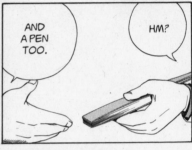

NO THANKS!

HUH?!

SENSEI, THAT'S MY MERCHANDISE. I NEED TO, UH...

HERE–A GIFT FOR YOU.

BUT EVERYONE WANTS ONE.

"NO THANKS"?

SKRTCH
SKRTCH

SO I CAN SIGN MY **OWN** AUTOGRAPH!

WELL, I'M A PRO TOO!

YOU RUINED IT!

HEY!

It's true, Hikaru. You really do have awful handwriting. Not like Torajiro at all.

JUST **LOOK** AT THAT!

THAT HORRIBLE HANDWRITING NEXT TO MY NAME!

LOOK WHO'S TALKING!

YOU SURE ARE DIFFERENT, KID.

You pay for it!

OH, UH... THANK YOU.

HERE, YOU CAN HAVE THIS.

188

The End of **Shinshodan** Series

Next Volume Preview

Hikaru and Sai are both scheduled for matches with their greatest rivals—
Akira Toya and his father, Toya Meijin! How will Sai play without revealing his
secret identity? And will Akira's father stand in the way of Hikaru's long antici-
pated rematch with his son…? The suspense is getting unbearable!

COMING OCTOBER 2008

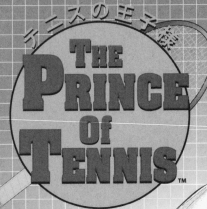

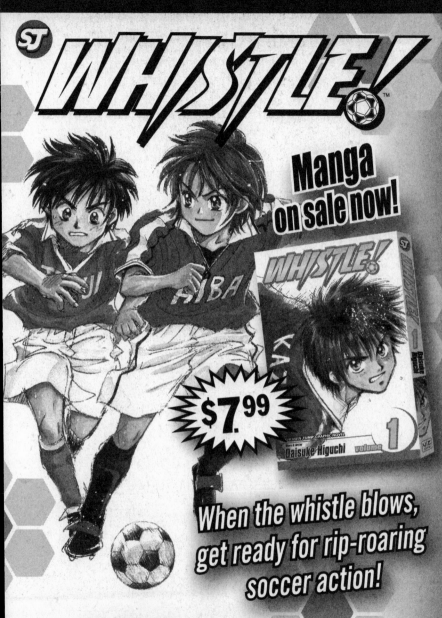

of contemplative versus practical Reason, 29–32; as symbol of human nature versus generation, 35–7; as symbol of Reason versus sense-perception, 22–7; as symbol of scientific knowledge versus its objects, 11, 16–17
maleness, 3, 5, 16–17, 22, 25–7, 32, 38–9, 51, 56, 92–3, 103–4, 106–8, 130
man, 5, 7, 11–15, 23–4, 27, 29–30, 32, 59–61, 65–6, 81, 83–4, 97, 99–101
marriage, 11–12
master-slave relation, 5, 16, 23, 88, 90–6
matter, 3–9, 10–17, 19, 22, 47; *see also* form-matter distinction
maturity, 66–7, 87
men, viii–ix, 3, 5, 11, 13, 15, 21, 25, 31, 48, 59, 64, 66–7, 69, 75, 77–8, 80–2, 84, 86, 92, 98, 100, 103, 107–9, 130
menstruation, 99
metaphors, 5, 7, 11–13, 15–17, 20, 39, 66–7, 128; *see also* symbols
method, 39, 40–6, 48–9, 51, 61, 116, 131
mind, ix, 4–5, 7, 9–14, 16–17, 19, 23–4, 26–7, 29–35, 39, 41–8, 50, 52–3, 69–70, 72, 75–6, 78, 84, 105, 107; relation to body, 6–8, 12, 17, 19, 33, 41–2, 45–7, 50; relation to matter, 4–6, 16, 47; relation to Nature, 10–17, 70, 72
morality, ix, 4, 27, 51–4, 58, 60, 62, 64, 66–71, 76–7, 79–85, 97, 105–6, 124, 130
mythology, 2–3, 5, 86

Nature, 1–2, 7, 10–17, 40, 42, 48, 57–66, 70–2, 77–9, 98, 101, 126, 128, 133; and Reason, 2, 10–11, 15–17, 57–65, 70–2, 78–9, 133; as moral exemplar, 58, 62; as woman, 11–12, 15–17, 59; domination of, 7, 10–13, 15, 17, 48, 57–8, 62; female, 29, 31, 84; female closeness to, 1–2, 16, 63–4, 77–8, 98, 126; human, 18, 24, 26, 28–31, 33–7, 39, 46, 51, 59, 60–2, 64, 125

Newton, Isaac (1642–1727), 58
Nietzsche, Friedrich (1844–1900), 1–2

oedipus complex, 69–70
opposites, Pythagorean table of, 3, 25, 131
Orphism, 6

particularity, 8, 21, 40, 42, 68–9, 71, 74–5, 80–2, 85, 88, 90–2, 95, 102, 105
passions, 6, 19, 20–4, 26–7, 33, 36, 46, 50–6, 68, 74, 77–9, 83, 132
passivity, 2–3, 24, 27, 51, 67
Philo (20 BC–AD 40), 22–8, 31, 75, 108, 114, 127
philosophy, viii–ix, 2, 13–16, 18, 37, 75, 87, 103, 105–10, 123–5, 130–2; history of, 103, 108–10, 131
Plato (427–347 BC), 2, 4–10, 12, 18–23, 26, 33–4, 39, 45, 50, 75, 126
power, 10, 13–17, 34, 50–1, 61, 66, 68, 80–1, 83, 92–3, 101
pride, 12, 15
principles, *see* universal principles
procreation, 21
progress, 17, 32, 57–60, 62, 64–5, 67; moral, 22, 26–7; of Reason, 58–60, 64–6, 70–1, 109, 133; scientific, 10, 57
public-private distinction, 44, 56, 67, 70, 74, 77–85, 87, 106–7, 124
Pythagoreans, 3, 6, 25, 104, 131

Ramus, Peter (1515–72), 42
Reason: and imagination, 46–8, 52; and Nature, 2, 15–17, 48, 57–65, 70–2, 78–9, 133; and passions, 19–22, 26–7, 36, 46, 50–6, 78, 132; and sense-perception, 6, 8, 23–7, 32, 46–8; inferior presence in women, 5, 22–8, 31, 36–7, 50, 66–7, 73, 75, 77, 103; maleness of, i–iii, 3, 16–17, 22, 26–7, 36–8, 50–1, 64, 75–8, 87, 103, 105–9; practical, 13–14, 30–2, 39, 46–7, 49–50, 68, 76; theoretical, 13–14, 30–2, 39, 41, 43, 46–7, 49–51, 68, 75–6, 78, 106

relativism, viii–x, 109, 132
reproduction, 3, 36–7, 125
rhetoric, 40, 43
Rousseau, Jean Jacques (1712–78), 57–66, 70, 71, 75–9, 84, 105, 128

Sartre, Jean-Paul (1905–80), 87, 93–102, 129
scepticism, 11, 72
Schopenhauer, Arthur (1788–1860), 77
science, 9, 11–16, 41–2, 47–50, 57–9, 61, 66, 75, 128
self-consciousness, *see* consciousness, self-
self-interest, 54–6, 79
sense, 5, 22–4, 27, 32, 46–8, 76; good, 43, 53
sense-perception, 8, 22–6, 32, 45
senses, the, 6, 8, 11, 23–4, 32, 34–5, 47–9, 68
sensuousness, 46–8, 50, 68, 75, 78, 89
sexual difference, viii, 5, 29–30, 67, 69, 105–6, 108, 127–8, 130
sexual equality, *see* equality
sexual stereotypes, 39, 104, 106; *see also* femaleness; maleness
slaves, 5–6, 12, 16, 19, 23, 90–2, 94–5
society, 54–5, 60, 62, 67, 78–80, 84, 91; civil, 54, 77, 79–80, 83, 85
Socrates (*c.*469–399 BC), 6, 19, 21, 39–40
Sophists, 28
soul, 5–9, 12, 17–23, 25–7, 29, 33–5, 40, 45–6, 61; divided, 7, 17–20, 22–3, 28, 45, 51
Spinoza, Benedict (1632–77), 51
spirit, 29, 31, 33, 71–2, 80–2, 88, 98
state, 1, 60, 67, 77, 83–5
subjection, 7, 12, 18–19, 23, 27, 30, 33, 89, 91
subordination, 7, 22–3, 28–30, 33, 36, 55, 64, 100, 106, 127
symbols, 2–3, 7, 11, 16–17, 22–37, 63–4, 74, 111, 114, 127; *see also* metaphors

theories of knowledge: as contemplation, 7, 9–11; as domination of nature, 2, 7, 10–13, 15, 48, 57–8, 62; as involving mind's transcendence of matter, 4–6, 12, 16–18; as power, 10, 13–17; as transcendence of the feminine, 2–5, 16, 37–8
transcendence, ix, 2, 4–5, 8, 10, 16–17, 21–2, 26, 37, 46–7, 50, 68, 71, 73, 80–2, 84, 86–7, 93–102, 104, 107–8
truth, viii–x, 3, 12, 14–15, 39–43, 45, 47, 49, 51, 57, 62, 71, 75, 88, 90, 108–9, 132–3

understanding, 11, 15, 50–3, 59, 68, 75
universality, viii, ix, 9, 38, 42, 69, 80–5, 105, 126, 132
universal principles, 42, 67–8, 70–1, 75, 130

virtue, 21–2, 27, 32–3, 55, 57, 63, 77–8, 81, 85; *see also* names of virtues

will, 32–4, 45, 50–1, 54, 98–9
wisdom, 19, 21–4, 42, 58–9
Wollstonecraft, Mary (1759–97), 76
woman, 1–2, 4–5, 7, 23–33, 35–7, 50, 64, 73, 76, 81–5, 87, 96–101, 105; as complementary to man, 23, 29–31, 35, 37, 50, 75–6, 78, 80–5, 87, 93, 98, 104–5; as other, 86–7, 96–7, 99; associations with Nature, 1–2, 11, 16, 58–9, 63–4, 77–8, 98, 126, 128; as symbol of generation, 25, 35–7; as symbol of passion, 26–7, 33, 56, 77–8; as symbol of sense-perception, 23–7, 32
women, viii–x, 2, 5, 21, 25–9, 31, 33, 35–6, 38, 44–5, 48–50, 56, 63–4, 66–7, 69, 75–82, 84–7, 92–3, 95–101, 103–8, 124–5, 127–8, 130
Woolf, Virginia (1882–1941), 74